THE
COCKROACH
INVASION

DR. SHERRY L. MEINBERG

THE
COCKROACH
INVASION

SKETCHES BY STUDENTS

A SCIENCE/MYSTERY BOOK
FEATURING THE
FURTHER ADVENTURES OF THIRD GRADERS IN ROOM 8

BY
DR. SHERRY L. MEINBERG

ARCHWAY
PUBLISHING

Archway Publishing books may be ordered through booksellers or by contacting:

Archway Publishing
1663 Liberty Drive
Bloomington, IN 47403
www.archwaypublishing.com
1-(888)-242-5904

Because of the dynamic nature of the Internet, any web addresses or
links contained in this book may have changed since publication and
may no longer be valid. The views expressed in this work are solely those
of the author and do not necessarily reflect the views of the publisher,
and the publisher hereby disclaims any responsibility for them.

Any people depicted in stock imagery provided by Thinkstock are
models, and such images are being used for illustrative purposes only.
Certain stock imagery © Thinkstock.

ISBN: 978-1-4808-0747-1 (sc)
ISBN: 978-1-4808-0748-8 (e)

Library of Congress Control Number: 2014910533

Printed in the United States of America

Archway Publishing rev. date: 6/25/2014

DEDICATION

To all of my students across the years,
that I have been lucky enough to know:
Even though cockroaches remain pests,
I hope you have gained respect for yet
another living species that shares our world.
Hugs and Kisses!

CONTENTS

CHAPTER 1

THE CRUNCHING PARTY

CRUNCH! CRUNCH! CRUNCH!

"AIEEE!"

"Bonsai!"

"Cowabunga!"

Much yelling and screaming could be heard coming from the Boys' Room.

CRUNCH! CRUNCH! CRUNCH!

"Take that!"

"Look out! One's getting away!"

"Stomp that sucker!"

STAMP! STAMP! STAMP!

A lot of movement and many voices were heard from inside the room. Much pushing and shoving was going on. The boys were being rowdy and loud. They were having *lots* of fun.

All of the noise and nonsense attracted a large crowd of students from the playground. Lured by the racket, the girls quickly came to see what the trouble was all about. They gathered around the steps in front of the doors to the Boys' Room.

"What's going on in there?" asked Velvet.

"It sounds like a *fight*," worried Willow.

"No," said Bella. "They're having too much fun!"

"It sounds like they're having a party in there!" agreed Emerald.

"They are!" shouted Ling. "Another CRUNCHING PARTY!" She always figured things out really fast.

"Ooooo!" many voices said together.

"Ugh!" added several girls.

"Yuck!" said others. Everyone laughed.

Even though the girls did not like CRUNCHING PARTIES, they were curious. They wished they could see what was happening. It sounded so exciting. But the Boys' Room was private. The girls had to wait for someone to come out and tell them what was going on. But none of the boys came back outside. They were having such a good time.

"There sure must be a lot of cockroaches in there," said Ling, as the girls nodded in agreement.

"Yeah," worried Willow. "This has been going on for a *loooog* time."

"There must be *hundreds* of cockroaches in there!" said Emerald.

"There must be *thousands* of cockroaches in there!" said Bella.

"Ugh!" laughed all the girls, dancing around together. Some of them made silly gagging sounds.

"*Millions* of cockroaches!" chanted the crowd.

"I'm glad those cockroaches aren't in the Girls' Room," said Willow.

"Me, too!" All the girls laughed.

A couple of boys came running up to the large group of girls surrounding the lavatory stairs. "What's going on?" they asked.

"A CRUNCHING PARTY!" some girls happily explained.

"Hot dog!" Zak was thrilled to hear the news.

"All right!" said Carson, as they high-fived their hands together.

"Hey, guys!" shouted Zak to some other third grade boys on the far playground. "Come on!" he motioned with his arm. "A CRUNCHING PARTY!"

"Big Time!" added Carson.

The boys let out wild-eyed war whoops, as they quickly ran to join the party. "Coming through!" they happily yelled, as they pushed through the crowd of girls.

"What's the battle cry?" a voice yelled above the racket.

"*Never surrender!*" a thunder of voices responded.

STOMP! STOMP! STOMP!

CRUNCH! CRUNCH! CRUNCH!

The boys were really getting rowdy. They were having a wonderful time.

Alerted by all the noise and commotion, the teachers on yard duty finally began walking towards the Boys' Room. "Uh-oh," several girls whispered, "Look who's coming!" Everyone knew that the teachers were going to break up the party. But just then the bell rang. RING! It was time for school to begin. Everyone quickly went to their classes. What an exciting way to start the day!

CHAPTER 2

THE INVASION

EARLY THE NEXT MORNING, ALL THE THIRD GRADE BOYS RAN TO THE lavatory. They had been looking forward to another CRUNCHING PARTY. But it was clean. There were no more cockroaches in the Boys' Room. It looked like all the cockroaches had been stamped out. Everyone was unhappy. The boys spent some time grumbling and complaining. Finally, they went back to the playground. They all found something else to do before school started. After a while, everyone forgot about the cockroach incident.

Late that afternoon, Room 8 was in the middle of a geography lesson. Ms. Matson was talking. The students were paying close attention. Suddenly, the quiet was interrupted by Emerald. "EEEKK!" she screamed. Everyone was startled. They turned to look at Emerald. She was standing up and pointing back at the classroom sink. She had a look of horror on her face. She just kept loudly screaming.

The whole class turned to look at the back of the room. A fountain of black was shooting up, spewing out of the sink. It looked like an oil geyser! It looked like a volcano erupting! No one could move for a second. Like playing a game of statues, everyone was frozen in place, as they gawked wide-eyed at the scene. There was a pause, as all were shocked, trying to figure out what they were seeing.

Suddenly the students realized what was happening! Ka-*jillians* of cockroaches seemed to be exploding out of the sink drain. UGH! The class went bonkers! The girls started screaming and running *away* from the cockroaches. The boys started yelling and running *toward* the cockroaches. Everyone was bumping into each other, as the cockroaches skittered and scattered, here, there, and everywhere. There was much noise and confusion in Room 8: total chaos.

STOMP! SPLAT!

"Another CRUNCHING PARTY!" yelled a few, with great glee.

"Hot dog!"

"Ya-hoo!"

"Cowabunga!"

CRUNCH! CRUNCH! CRUNCH!

"What's the battle cry?" shouted a lone voice.

"*Never surrender!*" yelled the rest of the class, in a flurry of activity.

"Ugh!"

"Ohhhhh!"

"Gross!" yelled the girls.

"Wait!" shouted Ms. Matson. "Don't stomp on the cockroaches! They will ruin our classroom carpet!"

"Ohhhhh!"

"I didn't think about that," worried Willow.

SPLAT!

"Yuck!"

Ms. Matson had a hard time getting to the back of the classroom. She had to dodge all of the students who were running every which way, as cockroaches scurried underfoot. She finally zigzagged her way to the sink.

No one could *believe* the amount of cockroaches that were shooting out of the drain. "OOOOH!" The noise level in Room 8 was getting louder and louder. There was much confusion. Everyone talked at the same time.

"Quick!" yelled Ms. Matson. "Grab some containers and trap the cockroaches!" She opened the cupboard doors and looked inside. She began to hand out empty jars, boxes, bowls, flower pots, and vases. Ms. Matson pulled out anything she could find that might hold some cockroaches. The students eagerly grabbed the containers, and went hunting. They placed the bowls and vases upside down, over the cockroaches. They trapped them *under* the containers, because those didn't have lids.

By this time, most of the girls, and only two boys, were seated on *top* of the desks. They were loudly directing the other students in their search.

"Over here! Over here!" they squealed, and squirmed, and pointed.

"No! It's getting away!"

"Watch out!"

"One's behind you!"

CRUNCH.

"Oh, no!"

"Eeeeewww!"

"He *squished* it! Zak squished it!"

"Oooooh!"

"Ms. Matson! Ms. Matson! Zak squashed a cockroach on our rug!" Bella tattled.

"I didn't do it on *purpose*!" yelled Zak.

"Yeah, it was an *accident*!" explained Carson, to anyone who was listening.

There was too much noise and confusion. Everyone was out of control!

SPLAT!

Finally, Ms. Matson ran out of empty containers. "Who is the messenger this week?" she shouted.

"Jamez!" several students shouted back.

"Jamez," called Ms. Matson. "Run to the office and tell them what is going on down here in Room 8. Tell them that we need more jars with lids! Then tell them to find the janitor. Tell Mr. Mayo that it's an *emergency*!" Jamez grabbed the Office Pass and was gone in a flash!

It quickly became clear that there were too many cockroaches, and not enough containers. "New direction!" shouted Ms. Matson. "If you have a jar or a shoebox with a lid, start *collecting* as many cockroaches as you can!" Most of the children began piling cockroaches into those few with lids. Those jars and boxes were quickly filling up.

The shoeboxes became a problem. Often, when a cardboard lid was lifted to put some captured cockroaches inside the box, other cockroaches quickly escaped. Sometimes more cockroaches got *out* than were thrown *in*! Some of the cockroaches had to be caught three or four times each. Whew!

Most of the students, and all of the cockroaches, were quickly moving around in one way or another. Twisting, turning, wiggling, and squirming. Chasing, racing, dodging, and jumping. Everyone added gleeful sounds to go along with all of the action. What fun for the class! What a *disaster* for the lesson!

At long last, the janitor charged through the door of Room 8. He stopped so fast that Jamez bumped right into the back of him. Mr. Mayo could not *believe* what his eyes were seeing! *How could a class be so out of control?* he thought to himself, as his mouth dropped open. Then he looked at the floor. *Oh, no,* he thought. *This is a BIG problem.*

"See, Mr. Mayo? I told you!" said Jamez, pointing at the sink. "Ka-*jillions* of cockroaches! More than you can count!"

Mr. Mayo was not a happy man.

RING! The school bell rang. It was time to go home. "Oh, no!" shouted the children.

"We don't want to go!"

"We want to stay here!"

"We don't want to leave!"

"Yeah! We want to *finish* the job!"

"We want to help Mr. Mayo."

"Please, please, please!" begged the children.

Saved by the bell, thought Ms. Matson. "Class, it's time for all of us to go now. I know you would like to continue to help, but I have a teachers' meeting that I must attend." Everyone loudly groaned.

"We'll leave Mr. Mayo to handle the rest of the cockroaches," she said, pointing to the sink, as even *more* cockroaches shot out.

"Shoo, now. Shoo, class!" Ms. Matson laughed, as she motioned everyone out of Room 8. "I want to thank each and every one of you, for all of your help this afternoon. And, don't worry, we'll finish our lesson tomorrow," she added, as she herded the last stragglers out. Ms. Matson shut the door firmly, and locked it. She waved a cheery goodbye to everyone, as she dashed down the hall to her meeting.

There was much grumbling mixed with laughter as the students skipped out of the building. "It's a bee-uuutiful day in the neighborhood...," several boys bellowed off-key, as others snickered and joined in. They all knew they had a GREAT story to tell their friends and family. *What an exciting day!* So they didn't want to hang around too long, anyway. They had news to spread.

CHAPTER 3

QUESTIONS, QUESTIONS, QUESTIONS

THE FOLLOWING DAY, THE CHILDREN WERE EXCITED TO TELL EACH other about the responses they got to their cockroach stories. Everyone had so much fun telling what happened when the cockroaches invaded Room 8. The students were giggling about what their friends and families had said. Many people had a hard time believing that *ka-jillions* of cockroaches would come out of the drain at one time. Other people found it hard to believe that cockroaches would come out in the *daytime*. Everyone agreed that it was a very unusual experience.

"Ms. Matson, why did so many cockroaches come out of the drain *at the same time*?" asked several students.

"I have *no* idea," said Ms. Matson.

"Well, why did the cockroaches come out *in the daytime*?" asked other students.

"I have *no* idea," repeated Ms. Matson. "I really don't know *anything* about cockroaches. I never even saw a live one before. I only saw them pictured in books."

The children found this hard to believe. They had all seen plenty of cockroaches before. The class grumbled upon hearing this response. They wanted easy answers.

"Well, how are we supposed to learn about cockroaches, if you don't know anything about them?" asked Zak. "Teachers are supposed to be smart!"

"Yeah, teachers are supposed to know *everything*!" added Carson, as everyone nodded in agreement.

"Now, just a minute, class," smiled Ms. Matson. "Remember what I've said over and over again: *Nobody* knows everything! That's why we have brains… so we can figure out what we need to know, *when* we need to know it." The class nodded their heads up and down. They remembered this speech. They had heard it before.

"I never had any reason to learn about cockroaches," Ms. Matson continued. "I've never been around them, so I never spent any time even *thinking* about them. Why would I?"

"Okay. Okay!" grumbled Tony. "We get the picture!" He wanted easy answers, also.

"So, are you interested in them *now*?" asked Scotty.

"Yes," smiled Ms. Matson. "I am *very* interested. I must confess that I am as curious about cockroaches as you are." The students grinned in satisfaction. They were curious, too.

"So," worried Willow, "where do we go from here?"

"Let's pool our knowledge," suggested Ms. Matson.

"What does *that* mean?" several voices asked at once.

"Well, let's all tell what we know about cockroaches," said Ms. Matson, "so I can learn, too. You each know *something* about cockroaches, so let's *pool* our knowledge, or *share* what we know with each other."

"Since I already told you that this is a subject that I know little or next to nothing about, you are going to have to tell me what you know. So I can learn, too," said Ms. Matson. "And I'll record your comments on this large sheet of butcher paper." She picked up a big, fat, black, felt pen, and wrote a title: THINGS WE KNOW ABOUT COCKROACHES.

Everyone was so excited, they all began talking at the same time.
"They're *icky!*" several girls said,
"They're *nasty!*" some children said.
"They're *gross!*" others said.
"They're *disgusting!*" added several other voices, as everyone laughed.
"Nobody loves a cockroach!"
"Everybody *hates* them!" more students shouted.
The class was in total agreement. Everyone was nodding their heads, all chattering at once. No one was listening.

"Class, class! Settle down!" laughed Ms. Matson. "One at a time, please."
The children eagerly raised their hands, while some waved their arms back and forth. Everyone wanted to be chosen to speak. Everyone had *something* to say about cockroaches. After it was quiet again, Ms. Matson pointed to the first speaker. "Velvet, tell us about something you know about cockroaches."

"Well, I know they're uggggg-ly!" said Velvet.

Everyone cracked up.

"Alriiiight!" Zak and Carson laughed, as they high-fived each other.

"That's right!" said several voices.

"They *are* ugly," agreed many in the class, as they giggled at Velvet.

Ms. Matson laughed, too. "Well, I tend to agree with Velvet," she sighed. "But remember, what is ugly to one person is not necessarily ugly to another. And what one person thinks is pretty, does not mean that everyone agrees with that idea of pretty." Everyone nodded.

"Just like babies," explained Zak. "Parents always think their own babies are so cute, but I've seen some really *ugly* babies…"

"Me, too," several agreed, as giggles erupted in the classroom.

"Yeah, some babies are all *red* and *wrinkled*," added Carson.

"That's certainly true," Ms. Matson continued. "I'm sure that a male cockroach would not think that all female cockroaches are ugly. Nor would a female cockroach see all male cockroaches as ugly." Everyone cracked up again.

"So, instead of using the words ugly or pretty, let's just *describe* cockroaches." Ms. Matson held up her big, fat, black, felt pen, ready to write on the large sheet of butcher paper, as the class was eager to share what they already knew about cockroaches. "What do we know about cockroaches?"

THINGS WE KNOW ABOUT COCKROACHES

(1)   Cockroaches are insects.
(2)   Cockroaches are black or brown.
(3)   Cockroaches have wings.
(4)   Cockroaches have bodies.
(5)   Cockroaches have six legs.
(6)   Cockroaches have heads.
(7)   Cockroaches have two eyes.
(8)   Cockroaches have mouths.
(9)   Cockroaches have two antennae.
(10) Cockroaches have brains.
(11) Cockroaches have hearts.
(12) Cockroaches have blood.

"Wow! Great beginning," said Ms. Matson. "Let's read through our list together." After everyone read the list out loud, she asked, "Is there anything else you can think of, to add to our description?" No one could think of anything else to say.

"All right, now let's think of things we know *about* them." Ms. Matson picked up her big, fat, black, felt pen again. She began writing as the children made suggestions.

(13) Cockroaches are pests.
(14) Cockroaches run very fast.
(15) Cockroaches are hard to step on.
(16) Cockroaches hide in the daytime.
(17) Cockroaches do not like the light.
(18) Cockroaches come out in the dark.

(19) Some cockroaches live indoors, especially in bathrooms and kitchens.

(20) Some cockroaches live outdoors.

"Wonderful!" praised Ms. Matson. "Now let's think of some questions that we would like to have answered. She wrote another title on a separate sheet of butcher paper:

THINGS WE WANT TO KNOW ABOUT COCKROACHES

I.   Why did the cockroaches come out of our sink, and not other classrooms?

II. Why did the cockroaches come out all at the same time?

III. If cockroaches don't like the light, why did they come out in the daytime?

IV. If everyone tries to get rid of them, why are there still so many cockroaches around?

V.   Why are cockroaches so hard to step on?

VI. Do cockroaches have ears? If so, where are they?

VII. Do cockroaches have noses? If so, where are they?

"Wow!" said Ms. Matson, as she quietly clapped her hands. "You have listed some very good questions. I'm impressed." She walked up closer to the class. "Now remember: If you think of any more questions, as the days go by, we'll add them to our list."

That afternoon, just before the bell rang to go home, Ms. Matson said, "Let's all try to find some information about cockroaches."

"You don't have to remind *us*," several children said.

"Yeah, just remember, *you* have to look for answers, too!" said others.

"That's right," smiled Ms. Matson. "We're all learning together."

CHAPTER 4

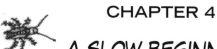

A SLOW BEGINNING

EVERYONE IN ROOM 8 WAS UPSET. THEY HAD BEEN LOOKING FOR BOOKS about cockroaches for several days. Nothing could be found.

"There are no books in our school library about cockroaches," grumbled several.

"Yeah! There aren't any kid books in the public libraries about cockroaches, either!" others complained.

"I know that cockroaches are icky, and all that, but *something* should be written about them," frowned Willow.

"I've looked, and looked!" Zak exploded. "And I'm tired of looking!"

"Me, too," added Carson.

The class agreed. They were all concerned about the lack of books written on the subject.

"Hmmm," sighed Ms. Matson. "Finding out answers to our questions is going to be harder than we thought." She was quiet for a short time. "Well, since there are no children's books about cockroaches, and we are just beginning to use computers, let's start with where we know we *can* find some information."

"Dictionaries!" shouted several children.

"Exactly right!" praised Ms. Meinberg. "Let's start our information search with dictionaries. Let's all use *different* dictionaries, and see what we can come up with." Each student quickly grabbed a dictionary, looked up the word, and copied the description.

Webster's New World Dictionary
cock'roach: an insect with long feelers and a flat soft body: a common household pest

New Scholastic Dictionary of American English
cock-roach: any group of insects, closely related to grasshoppers and crickets. Cockroaches are among the oldest kinds of living insects, and some kinds are common kitchen pests that live near water pipes and run mostly at night.

Funk & Wagnall Standard Encyclopedic Dictionary
cock-roach: any of a large group of swift-running, chiefly nocturnal insects, many of which are household pests.

"Good work," said Ms. Matson. "Isn't it interesting to see how short some descriptions are, and how lengthy others are." The students compared their papers with their friend's papers. "Now let's see if they all say the same thing. Everybody get your pencils ready." The students rummaged around, grabbing their pencils again.

"Ready for directions?" she asked. "We will cross off the facts we already know. Okay. Here goes: If your dictionary description says the word *insect*, please cross out that word." The class got to work.

"If your paper says *pest* or *pests*, please cross out that word," she continued.

"All right, if the word *night* or *nocturnal* appears in your description, cross it out."

"If your paper says *house, household,* or *kitchen,* or cross out those words."

"Next, let's look for the words *fast* or *swift,* and cross them out.

"And last, cross out the words *feelers* or *antennae.*"

"Now let's see what we have left. Circle the important words that are left in your description. Let's see if we have any new information."

Webster's New World Dictionary
cock'roach: an insect with long feelers and a (flat soft body); a common household pest

New Scholastic Dictionary of American English
cock-roach: any group of insects, closely (related to grasshoppers) (and crickets.) Cockroaches are among the (oldest) kinds of living insects, and some kinds are common kitchen pests that (live near water pipes) and run mostly at night.

Funk & Wagnall Standard Encyclopedic Dictionary
cock-roach: any of a large group of swift-running, chiefly nocturnal insects, many of which are household pests.

"Take a minute and compare your descriptions," Ms. Meinberg directed.

"Now, what have you discovered?"

"They don't all say the same things!" said several students at once.

"Wow! I never thought about that!" said Ling.

"Me, either," worried Willow. "I thought dictionaries all said the same thing." Everyone agreed.

"Just alike, but maybe a few different words...," said Velvet.

"Yeah, I thought dictionaries always said the same thing, but they were just made by different companies," said Jamez.

"Aha!" said Ms. Matson. "So why is this a good thing to know?"

"You can find out *different* information by looking in several *different* dictionaries. That's good to know, in case you're doing homework, and you don't have a computer in your house," said Ling.

"Or, like, if it's raining...," said Scotty.

"Or you're sick," interrupted Emerald.

"Or you're on restriction," added Zak.

"Yeah, *re*striction," nodded Carson, gloomily.

"... and you can't go to the library," finished Ling.

"Yes," smiled Ms. Matson. "If you read several different dictionary descriptions, you'll have a better idea of the subject. The same thing goes for books, magazines, and computer articles."

"Now, let me ask you this: Did any of the three dictionaries actually tell us the body shape of a cockroach?"

"Noooo," the class agreed, confused.

"Is it in the shape of a triangle?" asked Ms. Matson.

"Noooo!" the class giggled.

"A square?"

"Noooo!" the class chorused.

"Then what?"

"It's round," a few answered.

"It's like a circle," said others.

"You mean like a beetle?" Ms. Matson pretended not to know.

"No, like a stretched out circle," Emerald tried to explain.

"Ahhh, so what is the correct math term for that?"

"An oval!" shouted several students.

"Right you are!" smiled Ms. Matson. "Cockroaches have kind of oval-shaped bodies, but the dictionaries didn't tell us that. So, how did you already know what cockroaches look like?"

"We've all seen them," everyone said, in one way or another.

"Ahhh, you *observed* them, just like scientists," nodded Ms. Matson.

"Now, let's add the new facts to our list," said Ms. Matson, as she picked up her big, fat, black, felt pen. "What do you have left on your papers?" She added two more sentences on the chart, as the students directed:

(21) Cockroaches are related to grasshoppers and crickets.

(22) Cockroaches are among the oldest kinds of insects.

"Cockroach bodies are flat and soft," said Ling. Ms. Matson added those words to the chart, using a caret (^). She liked to use carets. A lot.

"And oval-shaped," laughed others.

(4) Cockroaches have ^flat, soft, oval-shaped bodies.

"Now why do you suppose that having a flat and soft body would be good for cockroaches?" asked Ms. Matson. "Why wouldn't they have hard, round bodies like beetles?"

"Flat bodies help them to hide more easily," said Tony.

"They can run under doors, and into tiny spaces with their bodies," said Velvet.

"With a soft body, they can squeeze under things, and into cracks," said Jamez.

"Good thinking!" praised Ms. Matson. She motioned to the class. "Cockroaches have *flexible* bodies. Do you have anything else to add?"

"My dictionary said *long feelers*," said Bella.

"Yes," said Ms. Matson, as she added another word to the Vocabulary chart. "Have you noticed that cockroach antennae are as long their bodies? Check out the picture. Their antennae are constantly moving. A cockroach cleans its antennae by pulling them through its mouth."

(9) Cockroaches have two ^long^ antennae.

"I have something!" Tony was excited! "We found out that cockroaches like to live around water pipes." Ms. Matson added that fact to the list.

(19) Some cockroaches live indoors, especially in bathrooms and kitchens, and around waterpipes.

Tony continued. "So, now we know why we were surprised about how many cockroaches there were coming out of our sink!"

"Yeah! There are always more cockroaches around than you can see," said Velvet. "They like to hide."

"That's true," said Emerald. "And no one ever sees pipes, because they are *behind* the walls and *under* the floors of our school.

"So we never realized how many cockroaches our school had, because we never thought about how many water pipes we have!" said Scotty.

"Just think about how many pipes this school has!" shouted Diego, getting into the spirit of the discussion. Diego was always embarrassed to speak during classroom conversations. "There must be *hundreds* of pipes!" he added. Everyone was happily surprised that he had joined the group discussion, since he was always so quiet.

"There must be *thousands* of pipes!" others added.

"Millions of pipes! Millions of pipes!" chanted the class. They were getting silly in their excitement.

"Possibly. Perhaps. Maybe. Maybe not. Now, let's think about this for a minute." Ms. Matson paused. " Do you think our school has hundreds of pipes?"

"Sure!"

"Yes!"

"Ab-so-lute-ly!" Everyone agreed.

"I think so, too," Ms. Matson said. "We have a *huge* school. How about thousands of pipes?"

"Yes!" The whole class answered at once.

"Each classroom has a sink…"

"And look at all the Boys' Rooms…"

"And Girls' Rooms…"

"And all the kindergarten rooms have lavatories."

"And the preschools…"

"And the Nurse's Room…"

"Don't forget the Teacher's Rooms…"

"And the cafeteria…"

Everyone was talking at once. They all had good ideas to share.

"Class, years ago, I read an article in the newspaper, that said our hill had 200 gas, oil, and steam pipes underground. If we add sewer and water pipes, there are even more underground. So, I tend to agree, if they are *short* pipes hooked together," said Ms. Matson. "Remember, our math word: *segments*? It could very well be that our large school has a thousand pipe segments connected together underneath our floors and the playground." All the children nodded to each other. "I just don't think we have *several* thousand. What do you think?" The class was quiet. The students were thinking.

"So, do you really think that we have *millions* of pipes? Remember what we learned in math: A million is a thousand thousands."

"Not really," said several voices.

"Noooo," said others, at the same time.

Many shook their heads slowly, from side to side.

"But it's so much *fun* to say," laughed Emerald.

"That's true," smiled Ms. Matson. "Just so long as you are aware that you are exaggerating."

"Millions of pipes, millions of pipes…" The students began chanting again, watching Diego join in with them. Just then, the bell rang. RING! What a fun way to go out to recess!

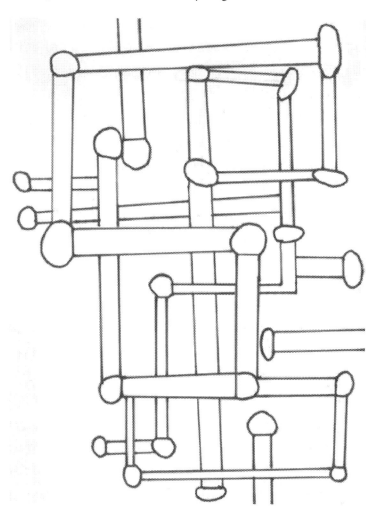

CHAPTER 5

ACTIVITIES

EVERYONE IN ROOM 8 GOT TO REPORT ON SOMETHING OF THEIR OWN choosing. Since some students liked the same subject, they gave their speeches together. All the students did their own research, and made their own charts. Some reports took longer to finish than others. But that didn't matter. They were not in a race. There was no rush. Whenever they were ready, they gave their reports. All were eager to share what they had learned.

Until the time when their reports were completed, the third graders were happy just to use cockroaches throughout their school days, in other ways. They had fun writing stories about cockroaches, and drawing pictures and diagrams of them. They spent a lot of time in math making up word problems for each other.

Bella

* If Ling had 5 cockroaches, and Tony had 3 cockroaches, and Willow had 2 cockroaches, how many cockroaches would there be in all?

(5 + 3 + 2 = 10 or 5 + 5 = 10)

* If Velvet, Diego, and Scotty have 3 cockroaches each, is the total more or less than a dozen?

(3 + 3 + 3 = 9 or 3 x 3 = 9, so 9 is *less* than 12)

When their cockroach reports were finally finished, the students were happy to share their research with the class. Everyone discussed the reports, and asked questions about them. All of the charts and illustrations were then placed on a special bulletin board. Ms. Matson added new facts to their classroom charts, after each report was given. In this way, everyone pooled their knowledge.

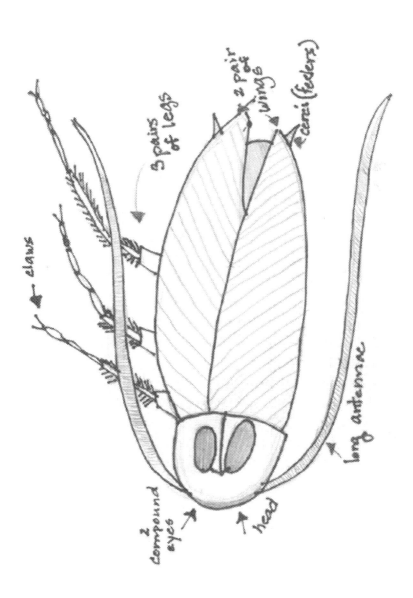

CHAPTER 6

COCKROACH HISTORY

TONY WAS VERY BRAVE. HE WAS THE FIRST TO GIVE HIS REPORT. HE showed his dinosaur diorama. Everyone knew that Tony loved to talk about dinosaurs, and were not surprised that he was able to include them in his cockroach report.

> Tony
>
> ### COCKROACH HISTORY
>
> Cockroaches are very old. They have lived on the earth for over 350 million years. They were here before the dinosaurs lived. They were here before the first people lived. Cockroaches have lived with people for a million years. They even lived in caves with the first cavemen. All throughout history, people have thought of cockroaches as pests. Fossils of cockroaches have been found from those long ago days. Those old cockroaches look very much like the cockroaches that live today. They haven't changed much in all that time. Scientists call cockroaches "living fossils."

The class clapped, and Tony said, "Some scientists say that cockroaches will be around after all the people are gone." This caused quite a discussion, with others adding their comments. The whole class got involved.

"You know, like WALL-E."

"Who?" asked Ms. Matson.

"WALL-E, the robot…"

"The lonely robot…"

"The movie…"

"WALL-E had a cockroach friend…"

"Yeah, his name was Hal…"

"Hal was a really good friend."

(22) Cockroaches are among the oldest kinds of insects, living over 350 million years.

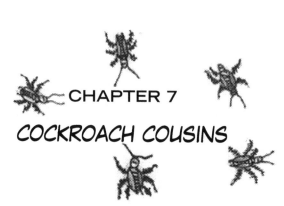

CHAPTER 7

COCKROACH COUSINS

VELVET WAS NEXT. SHE BROUGHT A GRASSHOPPER TO SHOW.

Velvet

COCKROACH COUSINS

Cockroaches are a part of a special group of insects. Their family name is called Blattaria. The insects in the group are larger than other insects. They also have a different kind of mouth. They have chewing or biting mouth parts. The funny thing is that instead of chewing up and down, they chew sideways, because their mouths open sideways. The insects in this special group are closely related to each other. They are like cousins:

crickets	praying mantis
locusts	walking sticks
kadydids	grasshoppers

After reading her poster, everyone clapped, as they tried to get their mouths to work sideways.

Velvet pointed to the last word, and added, "Some scientists say that grasshoppers don't belong in this special group, because they can *fold* their wings, and these other insects can't."

"That's right," Ms. Matson said. "Not all scientists agree with each other. They have different ideas. So they tell their theories to other scientists, and then try to prove what they say. Even when they *can* prove something, not everyone is convinced. It is a long process, to try to change people's minds." She paused for a moment.

"For example: Most scientists say that all the cockroaches in the world come from five families. But some scientists say *six* families. So they don't always agree." The students found this hard to believe.

"Wow!" said Diego. "I thought *my* family was big!"

(8) Cockroaches have mouths that chew sideways.

(21) Cockroaches are closely related to grasshoppers and crickets, katydids, and others.

CHAPTER 8

COCKROACH HABITAT

THEN JAMEZ WALKED UP TO THE FRONT OF THE ROOM, STRUGGLING with his butcher paper chart. It was so long, he was dragging it behind him. This caused a lot of comments from the class. Everyone knew Jamez was smart. He always had a lot to say.

Jamez

COCKROACH HABITAT

Cockroaches like to live in groups, and they are everywhere. They live all over the world. Most live in wild places, and have nothing to do with people. They are found in jungles, deserts, forests, fields, on farms, and in the cities. They share birds nests, large orangutang nests, bee hives, and tortoise burrows. They like to live where it is warm, dark, and damp. But they can live anywhere they can find some water and bits of food. They can even live in Alaska, as long as people are around.

Their favorite places to live are houses, hotels, apartments restaurants, grocery stores, and bakeries. They even live in hospitals and zoos. They can be found way down in the bottom of basements, cellars, caves, and mines. They can be found way up high in attics, and the tops of skyscrapers. They even ride up and down in elevators. They move along water pipes, steam tunnels, and gutters. They like to be around floor drains and leaky plumbing. Cockroaches especially like to live around motors, like refrigerators, freezers, hot water heaters, and other appliances. They also like radios, TVs, computers, electric clocks, and light switches. They travel anywhere that people travel. They ride around in cars, trucks, buses, trains, ships, submarines and airplanes. Most people don't even know that they have cockroaches riding along with them.

"Wow!" Ms. Matson said, after the class clapped for Jamez, "That's a lot of information!"

"Let me add some more history," she continued. "In the olden days, wooden ships often had *severe* cockroach problems. And cockroaches moved to and fro from country to country on cargo ships. For example: In the late 1500's, a very famous explorer named Sir Francis Drake, once captured a ship that was overrun with *millions* of cockroaches. And in the late 1700's, there was a very famous ship, called the H.M.S. Bounty. A

British Admiral, Captain William Bligh, was so upset by all the cockroaches on his ship, that he ordered his crew to disinfect the entire ship with boiling water." The class was amazed, but certainly understood the problem. "When some long-ago captains realized that monkeys liked to eat cockroaches, they allowed a monkey to roam freely on each of their ships, in an effort to control the cockroach population," she added.

"That must be why we often see pictures of a pirate with a monkey!" shouted Scotty.

"Good thinking!" clapped Ms. Matson.

"Could Columbus's ships have had cockroaches?" asked Ling.

"I've never read anything about that," Ms. Matson answered, "but cockroaches were common on *all* old wooden sailing ships, so I would imagine that Columbus had some cockroaches sailing along with him, too." She smiled, and added, "Even today, cruise ships and military ships have cockroaches as passengers."

"Ms. Matson, do you think that cockroaches are in spaceships?" asked Scotty.

"Actually, cockroaches have been launched into space in both high-altitude balloons and space capsules. Scientists have used them to study the effects of long-term space travel. *All* of the cockroaches survived in space, under extreme conditions," said Ms. Matson. "Even the babies. The Russians have done experiments with 33 cockroaches born in space, which were found to develop faster, and were tougher than those born on land. They are called Super Roaches!"

She took a breath, and added: "One cockroach actually hitched a ride on Apollo XII command module, which was noted on the mission log. I don't know if any cockroaches have set up house in the space station, yet. But you can be sure that they can, and they will, someday. Cockroaches have lived this long because they can *adapt* to any situation."

"Just like Hal," some students added.

"Something else I found out is that cockroaches like to live in *old* buildings," Ms. Matson said. "Older buildings are more likely to be infested."

"So they must really like our school!" said some.

"It's really old!" said Zak.

"Yeah, really old!" echoed Carson, as others nodded their heads up and down.

"How old is our school, anyway?" several wanted to know.

"It looks really old."

"That's because it *is* old."

"Way old!"

"Way."

Everyone looked at Ms. Matson, as she wrote 1924 on the board. "Let's find out," she said, as she wrote 2014 – 1924. "Do the math!" she said.

$$
\begin{array}{r}
2014 \\
- 1924 \\
\hline
90 \text{ years old}
\end{array}
$$

No one could believe that the school was 90 years old! When all the talking slowed down, she continued. "Our school has had three major additions, even before all the bungalows moved in. So the *whole* school isn't this old. But our classroom is, since we are a part of the original building." The students were astounded. They couldn't wait to tell their friends.

"No wonder cockroaches like our school so much!" said Tony.

CHAPTER 9

SIZES, COLORS, AND WINGS

Next, Ling shared her project with the class. Bella was her helper. "When we think of cockroaches, we think they are all the same," Ling began, as Bella and Ms. Matson passed out a plastic cockroach to each student. "We think they are all black, like the ones that shot out of our sink. And we think they are all about the same size. But, scientists say that there are close to *5,000* different kinds—or different *species*—of cockroaches." Ling took a deep breath, as the class tried to wrap their minds around such a large number. "Luckily, only 30 species like to live indoors with people."

"Well, I'm here to tell you that cockroaches come in all different sizes. They have different colors, and they have different patterns on their backs. Most have wings, some don't, and some have wings but don't fly." The class looked at her, wide-eyed.

"The world's *largest* cockroach is the Giant Cave Cockroach, that really has about ten different names. It lives in South America," Ling said, as Bella pointed to South American on the pull-down map of the world. "It lives a couple of other places, too, but only in the forests. It is a tree dweller. It lives in tree hollows and caves. It likes to climb up and down trees. It likes to eat eucalyptus leaves, fruits, and vegetables. It has *giant* over-sized wings. It is six inches long with wings that are a foot wide." She held up a six-inch ruler and crossed it with a 12-inch ruler to give the class an idea of how large they can be.

"Ooooooh!" The class was amazed.

"The world's *heaviest* cockroach is the Australian Burrowing Cockroach," Ling continued, as Bella pointed to Australia on the wall map. "It is also called the Rhinoceros Cockroach. Australia is the only natural place where it lives. It is three to three and a half inches long. It has a shiny brown, hard shell-like body, with no wings. It likes to dig underground tunnels to make a home to stay in. It also eats leaves, fruits, and vegetables. It can live from 10 to 14 years. It makes a good pet."

"That's as long as dogs and cats live!" whispered a student. Everyone was surprised.

"The world's *noisiest* cockroach is the Madagascar Hissing Cockroach. It comes from Madagascar, in the India Ocean, off the coast of South Africa." Bella pointed to the small island nation on the map. "I know you have all seen the cartoon movie Madagascar," Ling said. Everyone enthusiastically agreed. All had comments to make, since they had seen the movie, as well as both sequels. "Anyway, that island is the only place where it naturally lives. It also eats leaves, fruits, and vegetables. It keeps the jungle floor clean. It is a popular pet. It is also shiny brown, with no wings. Little mites like to live on this cockroach. When it feels threatened, these cockroaches will fight by crashing into each other. The males have two horns on their heads, just like goats. And they make loud hissing sounds. They live for only two or three years."

"So some cockroaches are as *big* as a computer mouse. Others are as long as adult fingers," Ling continued. The class was glad they didn't have to deal with such *huge* cockroaches. "But, there are also *small* cockroaches."

"Other cockroaches are much smaller than your plastic cockroach. Some are so small they can fit on a penny." Bella and Ms. Matson passed out a penny to each student. "And some cockroaches can fit on a little button." Bella and Ms. Matson passed out little buttons to everyone, as the class oohed and ahhed. "And some cockroaches are as small as an apple seed." Apple seeds were passed out to everyone. The students had a hard time believing what they were hearing and seeing.

"And that's not even the smallest!" Ling shouted. Her enthusiasm sure got everyone's attention. The world's smallest cockroaches are so tiny, they are the size of sesame seeds!"

Bella and Ms. Matson held paper plates full of black sesame seeds. They walked up and down the rows of desks. As each student licked one finger, and placed it on the paper plate, many sesame seeds stuck to it. No one could believe that the small black specks on their fingers could be the actual size of cockroaches. They shook their heads in wonder, as they compared the row of items on their desks: the plastic cockroach, the penny, the button, the apple seed, and then the sesame seeds. It was hard to think about cockroaches being that small. And the students said so, grunting in disagreement, disapproval, and dissatisfaction.

"Uh-uh!"

"You're making that up!"

"Not possible!"

"No way!"

"Yes, way!" Ling said, as she continued on, undisturbed by the class response. She knew what she knew. "These tiny cockroaches live in underground leafcutter ant nests. They ride on the backs of leafcutter ants. And they even fly on the backs of leafcutter ants through the forests." The grumbling continued. It all seemed so unreal.

"That sounds like make-believe!"

"That sounds like a fantasy!"

"That sounds like a fairy tale!"

"That sounds like a car*toon*!"

Everyone was talking at once. There was much whispering, movement, and eye-rolling from the students. *Could this be true?* they all thought, as each stared at the tiny sesame seeds on their fingers. After all, they had heard of leafcutter ants. Hmmm.

"Class, let's remember our manners," Ms. Matson interrupted. "Be willing to listen. Remain open to all possibilities." She paused a moment.

"Scientists suggest that the tiny cockroaches are fed by the leafcutter ants in exchange for their janitorial services. They keep the ants' underground tunnels clean. They depend on each other. No one really knows if they are treated like friends, or partners, or pets, or servants. And the tiny cockroaches have sticky pads on their feet, that help them cling to the ants' backs, when they are swarming."

"Although these cockroaches are much too tiny for us to see, the scientists that study cockroaches say this is true. And, of course, they have microscopes. It may be hard for us to believe, but it sure gives us something to *think* about. Right?" Heads nodded up and down all around Room 8.

"Remember, there are still people who think the world is flat. They refuse to think about any new information. So, put your brains in motion. Open your minds. Keep your wonder and imagination alive. Our motto should be: Keep looking, Keep reading, Keep seeking answers." And she wrote it on the board.

Suddenly, the room erupted with chanting:

"Keep looking. Keep reading. Keep seeking answers.

Keep looking. Keep reading. Keep seeking answers.

Keep looking. Keep reading. Keep seeking answers."

And a lone voice cried out, *"Never surrender!"* Everyone giggled.

Ling continued on, as if unbothered by the interruptions. "Most outside cockroaches stay near the ground, but some like to run around in the tops of trees. Others like to live some of their time *in* the water. They can dive and swim. They can stay *under* water for a long, long time. A lot longer than humans can." The class was clearly amazed. Imaginations were running wild.

Ling ended with: "Some cockroaches are large, some are middle-sized, and some are super-small. They come in many colors. Some have wings, and some don't. Some stay indoors and some stay outdoors. And they have different skills. Cockroaches are the same, and yet they are different. Just like people." And she bowed.

"Thank you, Ling, for a fascinating report!" said Ms. Matson, as the class loudly clapped for Ling. "It really gives us something new to consider."

CHAPTER 10

COMMON AMERICAN COCKROACHES

THE NEXT DAY, IT WAS BELLA'S TURN, AND LING WAS HER HELPER. They were very good friends.

"I am not going to tell you about all 5,000 cockroach species." Bella began. "This project is about the most *common* kinds of cockroaches in America." Ling placed the first poster on the chalkboard. "There are really six major species in America," Bella pointed, "but *I am* just going to talk about the first three, because they are so different."

Bella & Ling
THE MOST COMMON
AMERICAN COCKROACHES

(1)   The American Cockroach
(2)   The Asian Cockroach
(3)   The Madeira Cockroach
(4)   The Australian Cockroach
(5)   The German Cockroach
(6)   The Oriental Cockroach

The class read the poster together. Then Ling set the next poster on the chalk tray, and leaned it against the blackboard, as Bella began to talk again.

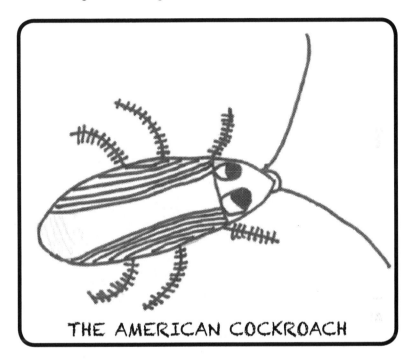

THE AMERICAN COCKROACH

"The American Cockroach is nicknamed the Palmetto bug or the water bug. It is the largest cockroach found in houses. It is large-sized. It gets as big as two inches long. It is reddish-brown, with a yellow edge. It has full wings, so it can fly short distances, but it usually doesn't. It stays outdoors." Then Ling placed the next poster on the chalk tray, as Bella began to speak.

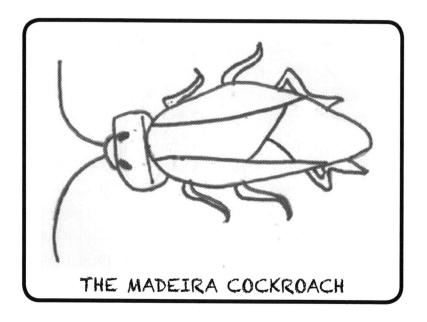

THE MADEIRA COCKROACH

"The Madeira Cockroach is also large, from one and a half inches to two inches long. It is a pale brown or an olive color. It first came from Africa," Bella explained, as Ling pointed it out on the wall map. "But it was named after an island in the Atlantic Ocean. It then came to New York, probably in one of those old wooden sailing ships we talked about the other day. It is very slow moving, so it flies a lot. If you bother it, it will feel threatened, and it will spray a bad smell, just like a skunk. Phew! It smells like something has died! Sometimes it even makes sounds." The students made expected comments, as Ling placed the next poster in the chalk tray.

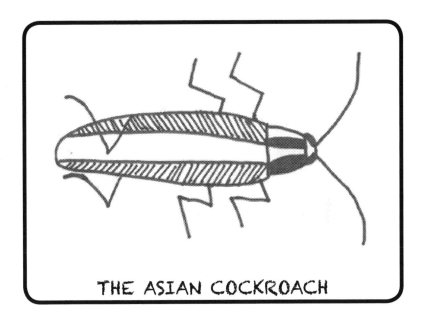

THE ASIAN COCKROACH

Bella began again. "The Asian Cockroach is also called the Flying Cockroach. It can fly up to 120 feet. It *likes* the light, and flies toward lamps and TV screens. It is different because it is not afraid of people, and likes to land on people who wear white. So look out! Asian Cockroaches like to be with other Asian Cockroaches, in large groups of 25 or 30. Can you imagine that many cockroaches *flying* at you, all at once?" she asked. The third graders all shook their heads back and forth in horror.

Bella pointed to her friend and said, "Ling and I found that every country has cockroaches. It's easier for people to say that they have waterbugs in their houses, than it is to say that they have cockroaches." Giggles erupted in the classroom. They knew it was true.

"Nobody likes to say they have cockroaches!"

"That's for sure!"

"I heard that!"

Bella continued on. "Each of the cockroaches has a different smell. And they all smell really bad!" More giggles were heard.

"Stin-ky!"

"Whew!" Some of the students held their noses.

"P.U. That stinks!" Others fanned their faces, while rolling their eyes.

Everyone got the giggles again.

Ling laughed as Bella kept talking. "Some people can even tell which cockroaches are around, just by their smell. Those people must have really good noses. But cockroaches recognize their family and friends by their special smells."

"Eeeewww!"

"Oh, gross!" several groaned, as sniffing was heard around the room.

After the class settled down, Bella said, hanging her head in sorrow, "It's so sad. We won't ever get to see the *pretty* cockroaches."

"Huh?"

"What?"

"What did she say?"

"*Pretty?*"

"Some cockroaches are quite colorful. They have brightly colored yellow, green, or red wings, just like butterflies. One species is totally bright green. Another is see-through, almost as clear as water. But they live far away, in the Rain Forests," Bella explained, as Ling pointed out where the rainforests are located along the equator. "The Rain Forests are warm and wet. They have plants, animals, and insects that are found nowhere else in the world!" This was certainly news to everyone.

Then Bella's finished her speech. "We didn't like all those cockroaches in our classroom, but it could have been worse. They could have been *bigger*, they could have been *flying* at us, and they could have been making loud, *hissing* noises and chirping sounds!" That sure got everyone's attention.

"Yuck!"

"Gross!"

"HELP!"

"At least we don't have to worry about *them*!" she laughed, as she bowed to the class. Everyone loudly applauded. All the students really liked the report.

Ms. Matson smiled. "What great examples both Ling and Bella showed us of comparing and contrasting cockroaches. We have learned a great many facts from their reports," as she grabbed her big, fat, black, felt pen, and began to write:

(2)   Cockroaches are mostly black or brown. **They can also be tan or olive, and even have colorful yellow, green, and red wings. Some look like beautiful butterflies.**

CHAPTER 11

WHAT COCKROACHES LIKE TO EAT

NEXT, SCOTTY SHOWED HIS POSTER TO THE CLASS. THERE WERE LOTS of comments, and more giggles, as the students read through the list together.

Scotty

WHAT COCKROACHES LIKE TO EAT

Cockroaches are not fussy eaters. They will eat all kinds of food. Anything people like to eat, cockroaches like to eat. They will also eat:

crumbs	garbage	dirt
wood	glue	ink
paste	shoe polish	paper
shoes	dead insects	books
dirty clothes	pet food	rugs
sheets	plastic	coffee
bedbugs	houseplants	blankets
fingernails	cat litter	leather
decaying fruit	toothpaste	soap
decaying wood	decaying leaves	

The group had a hard time believing that cockroaches would eat all those items on the list. After the class calmed down, Scotty gave his speech.

"Cockroaches are *scavengers*. You always see them running around with their heads down, because they are looking on the floor or the ground for food. They will eat almost anything." He pointed to the word toothpaste on the chart. "They will even eat flecks of toothpaste that you leave on your toothbrush."

"Eeeeewww!" groaned the class.

"Cockroaches love *onions*!" Scott continued. The class was astonished.

"Their other favorite foods are white bread, cinnamon rolls, boiled potatoes, bananas, and *beer*." No one could believe that, as they looked at each other in amazement. "Cockroaches also like meat, cheese, and grease. They do *not* like cucumbers, celery, hard-boiled eggs, or bacon, but will eat them, if hungry, and there is nothing else to eat."

Scotty had a wicked twinkle in his eye, as he continued. "They eat hair, eyelashes, and dried skin. They will eat dead insects, dead animals, and dead plants. They will even eat their own cousins, and sometimes other wounded or dead cockroaches. If they're really hungry, they will chew on the wings or legs of each other." The class went crazy! "And German Cockroaches will eat each other if they are too crowded together!"

Scotty waited for the uproar to quiet down, before continuing. "Although they don't eat very much at a time, they do drink lots and lots of water. Actually, they can survive without eating for *a whole month*, but they can only live *a week* without water." The students couldn't believe what they were hearing.

"*And...*" Scotty waited for everyone's attention again. "Cockroaches have *disgusting* eating habits. Every bit of food they walk on, they leave something behind. They walk on food with feet that are dirty from drains and sewers. They can spread diseases by polluting our food. They can spread harmful bacteria like Salmonella."

"Ooooo!" the class interrupted. They had heard that word before, on the news.

"Cockroaches vomit a part of the food they eat, and they spoil a lot of food with their own body wastes."

"*Vomit!*"

"*Body wastes!*"

"*Eeeewww!*"

"Gross!"

"Disgusting!"

"Yuck!"

Everyone was hysterical. Some were making gagging sounds. Scotty rolled his eyes, like he didn't know why the class was making such a fuss.

He waited. It soon became clear that Scotty wasn't done yet. His bright eyes and big smile gave it away. When everyone was quiet, he asked, "Have you ever wondered what happened to all the dinosaur dung?" And he waited again. When the class finally calmed down, he continued. "Scientists have studied fossilized poop, and found that ancient cockroaches ate it all up!"

"*Eeeeewww!*" the class responded.

"And today, some cockroaches eat the poop of bats and birds!" The class went nuts, as Scotty wrote the word **poop** in the last space on his chart. Wow! The things you can learn in a classroom!

Scotty coughed to stifle a snicker, as he bowed and sat down. Ms. Matson tried to keep from laughing, as she said, "Thank you, Scotty for the *interesting* information you shared with us, today." As she turned to the class, she said, "Since Scotty brought up fossils, let's review what we know about them." The class got ready to shout out the answers together:

Q: "How many ways are fossils made?"
A: "Three!"
Q: "How are fossils made?"
A: "Impressions, amber, and tar!"
Q: "How are impressions made?"
A: "In sandstone and limestone."
Q: "What is amber made from?"
A: "Sticky tree sap from ancient forests!"
Q: "What does tar come from?"
A: "Oil!"
"Great job! What good memories you have!" she praised.

Then Ms. Matson pointed to the word *glue* on Scotty's chart, and said, "Cockroaches like to eat the glue that holds books together. They also like to eat wallpaper, because that has both glue *and* paper." Then she pointed to the words *paste, paper,* and *crumbs.* "So you can see why cockroaches like to live in schools, libraries, and offices."

Pointing back to the word *glue* again, she said, "Cockroaches also like to eat the glue off the paper around the cans and bottles in your kitchen cupboards. They will even eat the glue off of postage stamps and envelopes. Many people used to use a wet sponge instead of their saliva, because they didn't like the bitter taste of the glue on stamps and envelopes. Others used a wet sponge because they didn't know if a cockroach had been there, and walked across the glue."

"Ooooh!"

"I never thought of that!" worried Willow.

"Nowadays," Ms. Matson continued, "Many postage stamps, return address labels, and envelopes, are already pre-moistened for you." Happy faces agreed.

"But some cockroaches still like to visit mailboxes and post offices," Ms. Matson said. "Oh no!" could be heard around the room.

CHAPTER 12

PROBLEMS

BIT BY BIT, AS THE INFORMATION SLOWLY CAME IN, THE CHILDREN found that not all of it matched. There were some big differences in what was printed as fact. The students became *outraged* that this could happen.

"How can we *believe* what a book says, if they all say different things? My book says that there are 2,000 different kinds of cockroaches," complained Zak. "But Carson's book says 3,000."

"Yeah! My book says 3,000!" agreed Carson. "That's a *big* difference."

"Well, my books says 4,500 different kinds," said Emerald. "How can this be, when Ling and Bella's reports said there were *5,000* different species?"

Everyone was upset. "Who's right?" could be heard a lot. It was hard enough to find information about cockroaches. And now they saw that the books didn't always agree with each other.

"How can be *believe* what the books say, when they all say something different?" worried Willow.

"Yeah!"

"Right!"

"How come?"

This was not good news.

"That is a *very* good question, class. You are really being observant," Ms. Matson said. "It's true. Just like our dictionaries, not all science and animal books agree with each other. A good way to understand this is to look at the *copyright date* of the book."

"What's *that*?" Everyone asked at the same time.

"Soooo glad you asked," laughed Ms. Matson. "Class, everyone take a book out of your desk. *Any* book will do." The students rummaged around in their desks, and took out a book.

"Now, everyone turn to the title page." Everyone did. "Now, turn that page over." Everyone did. "And now, look for a date on this page. Scan down the page, ignoring the words. Just look for a number. It should begin with a 19 or a 20."

"Found it!" was whispered around the room

"Have you all found it?" Some of the students had to help their neighbors. Finally they were ready. Everyone found the date.

"*That* date is the year that your book was published."

Everyone read the dates aloud to each other. "Now why do you think that the year is a good thing to know, when you are dealing with facts?" asked Ms. Matson.

The class was quiet. The students were thinking.

"I know! I know!" several children waved their arms to be called on.

"Because scientists are always learning something *new*," said Ling.

"… and doctors…"

". . . and inventors…"

"That's right!" beamed Ms. Matson.

"So a date closest to the year we're living in, should have the best information," said Jamez.

"Good thinking!" smiled Ms. Matson. "At an earlier date, the information in your books was considered to be true or accurate. So, at one time, scientists thought that there were only 2,000 species of cockroaches. Later on, scientists found even more types of cockroaches, so the books published after that, said there were 3,000 species. Much later, even more roaches were discovered. So now, newer books are telling us that there are 5,000 species of cockroaches."

"Soooo," began Zak, "does that mean that in a few years, new books might say 5,500?"

"Yeah! 5,500?" repeated Carson.

"Or even more?" several others asked.

"That might happen, because scientists believe that there are still *thousands* of cockroach species that have not yet been named. One scientist says that there might be *four times* as many still waiting to be discovered," Ms. Matson said. The class found this hard to believe. "How many would that be? Put your thinking caps on, and do the math." Everyone worked out the problem:

$$4 \times 5{,}000 = 20{,}000 \text{ cockroach } species$$

$$\begin{array}{r} 5{,}000 \\ \underline{\times\ 4} \\ 20{,}000 \text{ cockroach } species \end{array}$$

$$\begin{array}{r} 5{,}000 \\ 5{,}000 \\ 5{,}000 \\ \underline{+5{,}000} \\ 20{,}000 \\ species \end{array}$$

Heads were shaking back and forth. The number was too big to believe.

"Then again, maybe they won't find that many," explained Ms. Matson. "I'm just certain that *new* information will be added. Scientists learn more about animals and insects every year. Just exactly what that information will be, is anybody's guess." She was proud of her students. They were thinking for themselves. "We must remember that science changes as it makes new discoveries."

"Even knowing about book, magazine, and newspaper copyrights, I, too, am having trouble figuring out which is the latest information listed on computer website articles," Ms. Matson said. "The date and author is supposed to be placed at the footer, at the bottom of the web page site. Often, I can't find the author's name, the date, or whether the material has been changed, corrected, or includes the most recent information. For instance, one article says that cockroaches can hold their breath underwater for seven minutes, while another article says 40 minutes, and yet others say 45 minutes! Which do I believe?"

"Wow!"

"That's a looooong stretch of time!"

"That's confusing!"

"That's a *big* difference!" The class couldn't believe it.

"So, until we know what the latest information is, we'll just know that what Ling said is true. Cockroaches can hold their breath a lot longer than humans can."

"And while we're on the subject, let me tell you how science attitudes and ideas have changed over the years. And, Tony, you will appreciate this. Listen up, everyone!" Ms. Matson waited for attention, since some were still trying to hold their breath.

"Long ago, when I was in elementary and middle schools, all the textbooks pictured dinosaurs as *gray* in color. I used to ask my teachers how the scientists *knew* that dinosaurs were gray. After all, the only thing left of dinosaurs were ancient bones. So how did scientists know what color their *skin* was? I wanted to be convinced. But that was what my teachers had been taught, so they had no answers for me. Back then, dinosaurs were also considered to be quite dumb, sluggish, very slow moving, and cold-blooded. All the scientists and books said that dinosaurs were born alive, but that they were never cared for by their parents," Ms. Matson paused. "Now, is that the same information you have received from movies, TV, books, and magazines?"

"NOOOOO!" shouted much of the class.

"No way!" shouted the rest. They all began talking at once.

"That's exactly right!" smiled Ms. Matson. "Lots of scientific evidence has been found since those days, which has changed the way people think about dinosaurs. And, although there is much new evidence, we don't know all the answers yet. And, as I mentioned before, scientists don't always agree with each other. This is a very exciting time to be alive. Nowadays, new fossil finds are stretching our knowledge of such things."

"But maybe scientists thought the dinosaurs were gray because elephants are gray, and they are such *big* animals," said Jamez.

"Oh, Jamez, I thought of that, too, when I was your age!" Ms. Matson happily smiled. "And we might be right. Some scientists now are *still* thinking that the larger dinosaurs, at least, may have been gray, for several reasons." She counted on her fingers.

"Number one: Elephants have no need for camouflage, since they have no natural enemies. Number two: Elephants may be color blind, so there is no need to display bright colors to attract females. Number three: It takes way too much energy for bodies to produce spectacular colors. And number four: Elephants, hippopotami, and rhinoceroses, have trouble ridding themselves of body heat. And gray is the best color for heat balance in large animals. So those are four good reasons for scientists to reconsider the color question regarding large dinosaurs." Ms. Matson swept her eyes over the classroom. "Nobody knows for sure. So, it is *still* something to think about, isn't it?"

"And remember: Whenever you hear something new, listen carefully. Pay attention. Ask questions. Do the answers make sense to you? Be willing to ask: *How do you know?* and *What is the evidence?* If you are curious, or have doubts, check out the subject for yourself. Explore and examine such ideas. Look at things this way and that, up one side, down the other, and sideways. Make up your own mind. It is your choice. It is up to you."

CHAPTER 13

SOME ANSWERS

KNOCK, KNOCK, KNOCK!

Several girls were pounding on the classroom door.

"Ms. Matson! Ms. Matson!" called Velvet, before school began one morning. "Open the door! Please! I have the answer to one of our questions!"

The girls were dancing around. "Open up! Please, please, please," they begged.

Ms. Matson pushed the door open. "This is so exciting, Velvet. What did you find out?"

"I know why it is so hard to step on cockroaches! I know why it is hard to hit them with newspapers! I know why people often miss!" she shouted, jumping up and down. Several boys ran over to see what all the fuss was about.

"Velvet has the answer to question number four!" Emerald announced to the others.

"Alriiiight!" The class was *finally* getting an answer to one of their questions. This was taking a lot longer than anyone thought it would.

RING! The morning bell rang, but most of the students were already in Room 8. They couldn't wait to hear the news.

"Well," began Velvet, after everyone was seated. "Cockroaches have two special little tails, at the backend of their bodies…"

"*Two*?"

"Two *tails*?" The students had never heard anything like this before.

"Un-uhhh," could be heard around the room.

"You must be joking," a voice said.

"It's not funny," said another.

"No, really and truly. Their tails are not long, like the tails of dogs or cats or horses," Velvet explained. "They are tiny, tiny, tiny." Everyone tried to imagine it, as Velvet continued on. "I know it sounds weird, but they look like tiny triangles."

"Two tiny triangle tails," said Zak.

"Two tiny triangle tails," said Carson.

"Two tiny triangle tails," the class softly chanted. They liked the sound of it.

"What's even stranger is that those little tails can *feel* sound and *feel* movement."

"*What*?"

"What did you say?"

"You mean a cockroach tail can *hear*?" Scotty asked.

"Un-uhhh!" Many students shook their heads from side to side. Now this was just too much. Many frowns were seen around the room.

"No way!" said others. They were disappointed with Velvet.

"I don't believe it!" said a couple of brave classmates.

"I don't believe *you!*" others said at the same time.

The atmosphere was electric with tension.

"That *can't* be true!" someone shouted.

"It is so!" shouted Velvet, arms crossed and scowling. She was angry with her friends. They were interrupting! They didn't believe her!

"Now, wait a minute class," said Ms. Matson. "Calm down! Let's remember our manners. Give Velvet a chance to explain. *Don't close your mind to a possibility, before you've heard the whole idea.*"

"Anyway," began Velvet, staring hard at the class. "This little tail is called *cerci...*"

"Cerci, cerci...," whispered many. They liked the way it sounded. "Cerci."

The class was smiling again, as Ms. Matson added the word to their Vocabulary chart. So it must be true, the class decided.

"Actually their *two* tiny tails, are close to each other. Together they are called *cercus.*" The whispers continued, as Ms. Matson added the plural, cercus, to the chart.

Velvet continued. "Cockroaches use their cercus—their little tails—to *feel* movements of air. They can feel air moving, when other animals or people are nearby. This is a warning system, so nothing can sneak up on them from behind. This tells the cockroaches that they are in danger." She dug in her backpack, pulled out a paper fan, and started fanning herself. "It's just like when we use fans to move the air to keep us cool. We can feel the air move. Right?"

"Yes!" said some of the children, softly, nodding their heads in agreement. Everyone blew puffs of air onto their hands, or waved their hands next to their faces, so they could feel the air move, just like cockroaches.

"So," Velvet explained, "when a person's foot is coming down toward a cockroach, the foot pushed some air ahead of it. Or when a newspaper is coming down on a cockroach, the newspaper pushes some air in front of it. And this little bitty puff of wind is felt by the cercus. It is so fast, it happens just like this," and she snapped her fingers. The snapping of student fingers was suddenly heard all around the classroom.

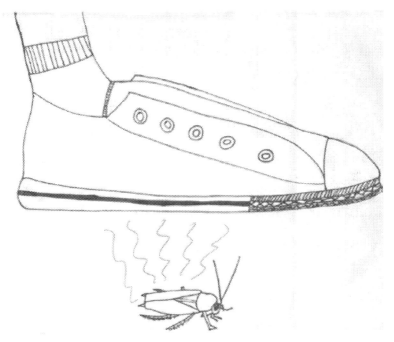

"Is that true?" Everyone wanted to know.

"Can that be right?" Everyone was talking, and snapping their fingers, and stamping on imaginary roaches.

"Yes," laughed Ms. Matson. "Thank you, Velvet, for sharing. Actually, it is even stranger than that. It is the tiny *hairs* on the cerci that get the message. The hairs are sensitive to air currents (or a tiny breeze), causing the cockroach to react. These little bitty hairs are connected to nerves. The message is sent from the nerves to other nerves in the legs. Then from those nerves on up the leg muscles. Then the cockroach starts to run. Cockroaches are very speedy runners."

"That sounds like it would take way too long," frowned Willow.

"It happens much faster than you can believe," Ms. Matson continued. "It happens in five hundredths of a second. That means that if you divide a second—and you all know how short that is—into five hundred parts, it would only take only one part of that five hundred, for the cockroach to feel the air, and get moving."

"Wow!"

"Cowabunga!"

"And, cockroaches have faster reflexes than humans," said Ms. Matson. "And, they can run over three miles in an hour!"

"No wonder cockroaches are so hard to step on!" said Zak.

"They sure are hard to stomp!" agreed Carson.

"Yes," said Ms. Matson. "They have built-in alarm systems at both ends of their bodies, that sense vibrations: antennae at the front, and cercus at the back." Everyone laughed. "I can't believe that you guys actually caught so many of them! It is very hard to surprise a cockroach." She rummaged around, looking for her big, fat, black, felt pen.

(14) Cockroaches can run very fast, **over three miles an hour. They can run faster than most humans.**

"But, if cockroaches have wings, why don't they use them?" asked Ling.

"That's a very good question, Ling. Most of the cockroaches

that stay indoors hardly ever use their wings. I guess they feel they are faster just using their legs, because they are more used to them. It's like the old saying about our muscles: Use it or lose it. We must keep practicing running, or we get so out of shape, that we can't run fast anymore. We have lost that ability to run fast, or run long distances. Cockroaches need to use their wings, to have them operate quickly. And there are some cockroaches that have wings, but they're not fully developed, so they can't use them anyway. Bigger species use their wings every day. Especially those that live outdoors."

"Should I cross out question number five on the chart? Do you all think you know the answer?" asked Ms. Matson. "YES!" shouted the class, with a mixture of cerci and hairs and wind and fast mixed in the message.

V.   ~~Why are cockroaches so hard to step on?~~

As Ms. Matson was crossing out the question with her big, fat, black, felt pen, Tony asked, "But does a cockroach really hear from its cerci?" He shook his head. "It just seems so weird."

"I know," laughed Ms. Matson. "I thought it sounded peculiar myself." She nodded at Velvet, and turned back to the group. "But according to my computer searches, the cercus help to keep cockroaches alert. Their six legs are also covered with tiny hairs, which gives them their sense of touch. Sounds can also disturb the hairs. Those little bitty hairs on their cercus and legs are so sensitive, they can detect the *footsteps* of another cockroach."

"Wow! So they can hear with their tails and hairs!"

(5)   Cockroaches have six legs, covered with hairs.

"In a manner of speaking...," said Ms. Matson. "They *sense* noise instead of actually hearing it as humans do, but it's close enough."

"Let's cross that question off of our chart, too," said Bella.

"Yeah!" agreed the others.

"Okay. We now know that a cockroach senses sound through hairs on its cerci." And she crossed question number five off the list, with her big, fat, black, felt pen.

VI. ~~Do cockroaches have ears? If so, where?~~

"And actually," continued Ms. Matson, "I found *another* funny fact you might be interested in, as well." The class was hanging on every word. "What are the antennae for?"

"To feel with," many students answered.

"Cockroaches use their antennae to *touch* things in the dark," said Zak.

"That's why they're called *feelers*, because they *feel* things," added Carson.

It was clear that everyone knew the reason for feelers. "You are all right. But there is something else that cockroach antennae are for," she smiled. "You'll never guess. They also *smell* with their antennae."

"What...?"

"Are you joking?" The class started giggling.

"They *smell* with their feelers?"

Everyone laughed. They were having a grand time.

But Ms. Matson had a funny look on her face. She hadn't told them everything, the class could tell. She was almost bursting with the news.

"You know something else…," said several.

"Come on, tell us…," begged some.

"Please, please, please…," the class begged. "We can't wait forever."

Ms. Matson grinned. "All right," she said. "You've twisted my arm. I can't keep this secret any longer. It's just too unusual."

The class clapped and cheered. "Okay," said Ms. Matson. "We now know that cockroach antennae are for feeling and for smelling. They are also for *tasting*!"

"No way!"

"Un-uhhh! You can't trick us!"

"You're making this up."

"No, no. This is really and truly a fact," laughed Ms. Matson, as she grabbed the pen again. "A strange fact, but a fact nonetheless."

(9)   Cockroaches have two long antennae, **for feeling, smelling, and tasting.**

"What about question number seven?" asked Ling.

"Draw a line through that one, too!" said Zak.

"Yeah! Cross it out!" added Carson.

"Now wait just a minute," laughed Ms. Matson. "Let's be careful here. What does number six say? Everyone, let's read the question out loud together," as she pointed to the chart.

"Do cockroaches have noses? If so, where?" the class read aloud.

"Do we know the answer to that question?" she asked.

"Sure we do!"

"Yes!"

"You just told us the answer!"

The children were looking confused.

"Now think for a minute," Ms. Matson directed. "What did we say that antennae do?"

"They feel, they taste, and they smell!"

"Okay. What does your nose do besides smell?" she asked.

"Breathe!" many voices called out.

"We breathe through our noses."

"Our noses are to breathe *and* to smell with."

"Right you are!" Ms. Matson smiled. Everyone looked at each other. Some shrugged their shoulders. All were confused. "I said that the antennae smell. Did I say antennae *breathed*?" The class was quiet for a minute. Thinking.

"They don't breathe with their feelers?"

"They just smell with their feelers?"

"Cowabunga!" The room suddenly broke into loud talking.

"Cockroaches are sooooo interesting!" Diego forgot his shyness, and said what everyone was thinking.

"I was messing with your minds. I'm sorry that I teased," Ms. Matson apologized. But somehow she didn't look sorry. She was laughing. "Okay. Okay. Let me explain. Cockroaches smell with their feelers. But they don't have noses like humans. They breathe through 20 holes in their bodies. There are four holes on their back, and 16 holes along the edge of their bodies." The class was looking wide-eyed. "You know, just like whales have a blow-hole on their backs…" The students nodded. "Just like that, or like our two nostrils, only they have more little holes, called *spiracles*."

"Spiracles, spiracles, spiracles," was whispered about.

"So, what three things are cockroach antennae for?" Ms. Matson asked.

"They *feel*, they *taste*, and they *smell!*" Everyone cheered. They got that right.

"So, do cockroaches have noses?"

"NOOOO!" everyone shouted. "They use their feelers as noses."

"Well, then, how do they breathe?" she asked again.

"They have some little holes…"

"The breathe through 20 holes in their bodies."

"Their bodies have tiny holes…"

"I think you've got it!" Ms. Matson gave the class a thumbs-up sign. Then she went to her desk, and picked up her big, fat, black, felt pen. She drew a wiggly line through question number seven. The class applauded. For days, they had not one single answer to their questions. And now, in one day, they knew the answers to *three*.

VII. ~~Do cockroaches have noses? If so, where?~~

This was too much. What an unusual insect! Cockroaches hear with their tails. They smell and taste with their antennae. They breathe through a bunch of holes in their bodies. Triple strange.

On the way home from school that afternoon, Zak shook his head. "I don't think anybody is going to believe this," he said sadly.

"Yeah," agreed Carson. "Convincing people is going to be hard work."

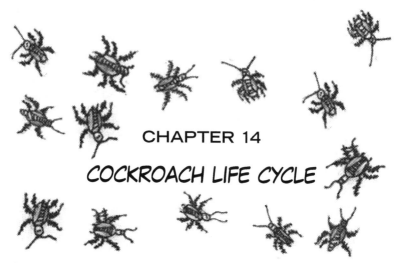

CHAPTER 14

COCKROACH LIFE CYCLE

Before school one morning, Mr. Mayo stopped Ms. Matson in the hall. He looked upset.

"Just what kind of a *crazy* class are you teaching?" he demanded.

"What do you mean?" asked Ms. Matson. She was surprised. She couldn't imagine what had made him so grumpy.

"Every day your students *bother* me about cockroaches!" he complained. "They're always pestering me with new facts they learned."

"But that's wonderful!" she beamed. Ms. Matson was very pleased to hear this news. "Not only are they remembering what they are learning, but they want to share it with you! After all, you *were* a part of our cockroach invasion." She smiled.

"Well...," Mr. Mayo said. He didn't know quite what to say.

"They are just excited about what they are learning. And, because they like *you*, they want you to know, too," she explained further.

"Well...," Mr. Mayo thought some more. "I just thought everyone was *blaming me* for all of the cockroaches."

"No, no...," Ms. Matson began. "That thought never even came up! It never even crossed their minds. No one is *blaming* anyone. Actually, they see you as rescuing our classroom from all those pests."

"Well...," He thought some more. "If you're sure about that, then I won't let it trouble me anymore."

They waved to each other, as they went off in different directions. They both had smiles on their faces.

Most of the students in Room 8 were finishing up their projects. Many new facts were being added to the classroom charts. The class couldn't believe that they had learned so much about cockroaches. They enjoyed sharing all the new information with their friends and family members.

Four students—Willow, Emerald, Zak, and Carson—made posters showing the life cycle of cockroaches. They presented their posters, and talked to the class about what they knew.

Emerald started talking first. "Cockroaches live longer than most insects. The lifetime of a cockroach depends upon the species. A few only live for a couple of months. Most live to be between one and three years. But remember what Ling told us? The Australian Burrowing Cockroach can live 10 to 14 years!"

"The Madagascar Hissing Cockroach is the only known cockroach to give live births. The rest lay eggs. When the female cockroach is ready to lay eggs, she makes sure that she is all alone. Then she will begin to lay eggs."

Willow stepped forward. "The mother cockroach will lay anywhere between 12 to 45 eggs, in two rows. She has them in a special container. It is called by many names. Scientists call the container ootheca." Everyone gigged and rolled their eyes. "But it is also called an egg pack, or an egg sac, or an egg pouch, or an egg case, or an egg bag, or an egg purse," she explained. "But they all mean the same thing. It is a little container to hold the eggs. It protects the eggs, and keeps them from drying out. Cockroach eggs containers look kind of like our egg cartons, two by two. Or a six-pack of soda, two by two. Only more. And real tiny." The class giggled.

"The egg purse looks like a long vitamin pill," added Emerald.

"Like a capsule?" asked Ms. Matson.

"Yes, just like an aspirin capsule," agreed Willow, as she pulled one out of her pocket to share. She almost forgot to show it. Emerald nodded her head up and down, as she showed her picture. Ms. Matson wrote ootheca on the chart.

"Some cockroach species just drop the egg purse wherever they are, and leave it behind. Others hide the egg purse in safe places. And some will carry the egg purse around with them, until the eggs hatch," said Emerald. "If the cockroach keeps her eggs with her, she has to carry them around from four weeks to eight weeks. The egg pack sticks to her body. She uses some kind of special paste or glue to attach it to her body, so the egg purse never falls off."

"Then," said Willow, "when the eggs are almost ready to hatch, she will leave the egg purse in a dark, safe place. Then she just goes on her way. She doesn't take care of them anymore."

Emerald explained further. "It takes from four to 12 weeks for the eggs to hatch. The egg purse has tiny holes in it, so the babies can breath. When they get bigger, the baby cockroaches struggle to get out of the purse, just like baby birds pushing to get out of their eggs. When the babies get too big for the egg purse, they hatch when the egg purse splits open at the top. It opens up just like a purse with a zipper." She grabbed her own purse, and zipped it open. "Then they all wiggle out," she said, as she demonstrated with her hand: wiggle, wiggle, wiggle. Everyone wiggled their hands.

"They look just like their parents, except they are white, and they don't have their wings yet. They are called *nymphs*," Willow explained.

"Nymphs, nymphs…," the class whispered. That was a hard word for some of them to say. Ms. Matson added the word to the class Vocabulary chart.

"They are very fast, even though they are babies," added Willow. "Then they just zip away and search for crumbs or something to nibble. Nobody has to teach them anything. They already know what to do. And a few hours later, their skin turns from white to dark." Both girls stepped back.

Next, Zak and Carson started their part of the project. They continued to talk about the life cycle of cockroaches.

"Then the baby cockroach…," said Carson.

"The *nymph*…," suggested Zak.

"Then the nymph grows until its skin gets too tight. Then it sheds its old skin, just like a snake sheds its skin. It's just like when we grow older, we need bigger coats."

"It's called *molting*," explained Zak. "It *molts*."

"Molts, molting…," whispered the class. They were learning several new words today. They were trying to keep them clear in their minds.

"Anyway, the nymph wiggles out of the old skin," Carson said, as he wiggled his body, "and the new skin is soft and white again. But after eight hours it turns hard and dark. It returns to its regular color. So, if you see a white cockroach, it is not an albino. It has just shed its skin, because it needs a bigger size."

"Sometimes, a nymph will *eat* its old skin!" Carson yelled in excitement.

"Eeeeyooou!" the class groaned together.

"Gross!" Everybody laughed, as Carson rolled his eyes, and pretended to eat his skin. "Mmmmm, good!" he said, smacking his lips.

"Yuck!" Others said, as they watched him. They couldn't imagine eating their own skin.

"This molting happens over and over," said Zak. "The nymph gets bigger every time it molts. Its body doesn't change, just its size. Weeks and weeks go by, and it molts six to 12 times. The nymph keeps getting bigger and bigger. And its wings finally begin to appear."

Then it was Carson's turn. "After almost a year, it molts for the last time. When the skin splits open, a full-grown cockroach wiggles out."

"Eeeeyooou!" the girls chorused.

"Cool!" said Tony.

"Cockroaches are all grown up when they are just a year old?" Ling was shocked. "It takes 21 *years* for us to become adults." Lots of whispering could be heard around the room.

"That's right!" answered Zak. "When they are about one year old, the female cockroaches start laying their own eggs."

"Wow!" said Bella.

"Yeah, and that's not all!" answered Zak. The two boys looked at each other and grinned. "Now comes the part that you really won't believe!"

"That's right," said Carson. "You won't believe it!"

"Tell us, tell us," several chanted.

"Hurry," begged others.

"Are you ready?" asked Zak. Everyone nodded their heads up and down.

"One American Cockroach can lay around *one hundred fifty eggs* in one year!" shouted Zak.

"What?"

"They can have 150 babies…"

"… in one *year?*"

Everyone was talking at once. This was unbelievable.

"And," added Zak, "if all of those nymphs hatched, and they start having babies, they can have about 70,000 babies *altogether*, in one year."

"70,000 babies!"

"In one year?"

"I don't believe it!"

The class was amazed.

"No wonder people can never get rid of them!" said Velvet.

"That's way too many babies," worried Willow.

"No way!" agreed Jamez.

"That's unbelievable!" said Ling.

"It's a good thing we can't see them all," said Velvet, as she shivered.

"It gets even worse," yelled Zak. "The German Cockroach only lives about one hundred days, but it can lay *one million* eggs Suddenly, the class started chanting, "Millions, and millions, and millions of cockroaches!"

To sum up their project, Zak said: "Cockroaches can be brought into your house in boxes, bags, suitcases, and furniture. Even in clothes. All it takes is *one* little egg capsule," as Willow showed her aspirin capsule again, "and six months later, your house will be *crawling* with roaches."

"And that's called an *infestation*," Ms. Matson added. "Your house would be *infested* with cockroaches," as she wrote the word on the Vocabulary chart.

The four students stood shoulder to shoulder, and said the last sentence together: "Then the life cycle starts all over again: Eggs, nymphs, adults; Eggs, nymphs, adults." The class picked up the pattern, and easily chanted together, "Eggs, nymphs, adults," repeating it several times. Then Emerald, Willow, Zak, and Carson held hands and bowed together. The class loudly clapped. It was clear that everyone enjoyed listening to what other students had to say about their projects. Cockroaches might be icky, but they sure were interesting.

CHAPTER 15

COCKROACH ENEMIES

AT LONG LAST, ALL BUT ONE HAD PRESENTED THEIR PROJECTS. SOME were long, and some were short. It didn't matter, because the students learned something with each report. But everyone knew who would give the shortest speech of all: Diego. He was nervous as he placed his poster on the chalk tray.

Diego

COCKROACH ENEMIES

birds	frogs	snakes
spiders	toads	wasps
centipedes	mice	rats
geckos	bats	ants
lizards	scorpions	people

Diego was shy. Diego was embarrassed. Diego didn't like standing in front of the class. And he didn't certainly didn't like everyone staring at him. Everyone knew that, so they smiled at him so he would feel comfortable. After swallowing, and clearing his throat several times, he stiffly pointed to his poster, and everyone read it out loud together.

Then Diego began: "Cockroaches have lots of enemies. But the cockroaches run so fast, and they hide so well, it is hard for their enemies to find them. Some cockroaches can even tuck their legs underneath them, and lie flat like turtles, to protect themselves. Some cockroaches spray a smelly, burning mist at enemies. Other cockroaches can shoot out a kind of glue that sticks to the legs of ants and beetles, stopping them from attacking. Some people keep geckos for house pets, to catch cockroaches at night. Some cats kill cockroaches, but other cats just play around with them, and then let them go. So I didn't put cats on my chart. And some animals don't like to *smell* the cockroaches, so they just leave them alone. Stinky!" he explained, holding his nose, as the class laughed.

"Frogs and toads can catch cockroaches by sitting real still, and letting their long tongues reach out and grab them." Diego demonstrated by standing still, and sticking his tongue in and out, in and out, as the students giggled. Suddenly everyone was sticking their tongues in and out, in and out. "And some wasps like to carry cockroaches into their nests, as food for their babies. Yum-yum!"

"Eeeewwww!" the class groaned, making faces at each other, as they happily clapped their hands for Diego.

Later that afternoon, when the class was lined up in single file to go home, Ms. Matson said, "I have something interesting for you to share with your families. She waited to have everyone's attention, and then opened her hand. "What is this? What am I holding in my hand? Does anyone know?"

"*Garlic!*" everyone shouted. All were curious as to why their teacher would show them garlic. This wasn't a cooking class.

"Right you are," she smiled. "This whole garlic, with roots and all, is called a garlic *head*, or a garlic *bulb*. There are several types of garlic, but this is the most common. It is called a white-skinned garlic. The white papery outside is called the *skin*. So, when you unwrap the papery outsides, or you peel off the skin…," she demonstrated, "you will find what are called *buds*, or more often, *cloves*. See?" Everyone nodded.

"These buds, or cloves, are used in cooking, in many different ways, all over the world. And they can be made into flakes, powder, juice, and salt," as she held up a small jar of garlic salt for everyone to see.

The words garlic, head, bulb, buds, and cloves, were whispered around the room. The students knew that Ms. Matson was making a point about something, and they wanted to follow her thinking. "Now hold out your hand," she directed, as she walked down the line, and dropped a garlic bulb into their palms. "You can teach your family something new about garlic tonight."

"Learning about cockroach *history*," she smiled at Jamez, "and learning about cockroach *enemies*," she smiled at Diego, "I have something else to add."

"Long ago, people believed that garlic was a good way to get rid of cockroaches. Actually, people today *still* use garlic as a *natural* way to make cockroaches go away. Cockroaches don't like extremely strong smells, which is funny because animals and people think cockroaches smell *really* bad. And garlic is a powerfully *strong* odor for cockroaches. So cockroaches don't like to be around garlic. At all." Loud sniffing could be heard, as the class breathed in the scent, making appropriate responses.

"So people simply put cloves of garlic in places where cockroaches have been seen, to keep them from returning. Other people create a spray, by mixing water and garlic together, and spraying areas where cockroaches have been."

After the students calmed down, Ms. Matson said, "Now help me remember, class. Put on your thinking caps," as she paused, tapping her forehead. "For hundreds of years, garlic was used to get rid of cockroaches, lice, and... what else?"

"VAMPIRES!" the students screamed in response, as they charged out the door, laughing. School was *soooo* much fun.

CHAPTER 16

GETTING RID OF COCKROACHES

THE NEXT DAY, EVERYONE HAPPILY SHARED THEIR FAMILIES' REACTIONS TO the garlic bulbs. Then they discussed other *natural* ways to get rid of cockroaches, like catnip, bay leaves, cucumber, and Osage orange oil. Finally, Ms. Matson said, "Let's read Question IV together."

The students read aloud: "If everyone tries to get rid of cockroaches, why are there so many around?"

"Good reading," said Ms. Matson. "I think we learned part of this answer the other day. Who can help us with this?" Hands were raised all around the room.

"We found out that the female cockroach lays *way* too many eggs," said Willow.

"And they *hide* their eggs too well," added Ling.

"Too many baby cockroaches are hatched in a short time," said Scotty.

"All true," praised Ms. Matson. "Anything else?"

"Another reason is that cockroaches don't have enough enemies," said Tony.

"And cockroaches are *speedy*," said Jamez. "They are too fast to be caught by many of their enemies."

"They have to be *smart*," said Zak. "The couldn't have lived for millions of years if they were stupid."

"Yeah, they can *adapt*," said Carson. Everyone turned and stared at him. No one was used to hearing big words out of his mouth. He was usually like a parrot, copying what everybody else said. Especially Zak. "What?" he asked the group, holding his arms out, as if to say, *What did I do?*

"Oh, good," praised Ms. Matson. "Let's add that to number 10, as she grabbed her big, fat, black, felt pen, to add some words. "Thank you, Carson."

10.   Cockroaches have tiny brains, but **they can learn and adapt quickly.**

"Those are all good reasons," said Ms. Matson. "Now, let's review. What do most people do to try to get rid of cockroaches?"

"Ooh! Ooh! Ooh!" Everyone raised their hands. They all had something to say:

"One way is to *starve* them out."

"Keep your food in sealed containers."

"You don't leave any crumbs laying around."

"You don't leave dirty dishes out."

"Yeah, you wash your dishes immediately."

"You sweep the floors."

"Keep pet food and water on a mat."

"Or put pet bowls on a raised wire tray."

"Don't overwater house plants, and leave standing water for cockroaches."

"Empty the trash often. Don't let it overflow."

"Keep a lid on your garbage can."

"You fix leaky faucets right away."

"Keep your whole house clean."

"Good answers!" said Ms. Matson. "That's what most people try to do. But that isn't always successful. The *cleanest* houses in the world can still have cockroaches. Why is that?"

"There are cracks and little spaces for cockroaches and other insects to crawl inside," said Jamez.

"Right," agreed Ms. Matson. "So people need to seal up the cracks in their floors, and walls, and roofs."

"Because," shouted Tony, "they don't just eat *food*. Look at our chart. Cockroaches eat *any*thing and *every*thing!" The class giggled at Tony's excitement.

"And," added Velvet, "they don't eat very much. They can go for one whole month without food, and one week without water, so it doesn't bother them."

"Yeah, as long as they have some water, they can go without food for a long, long time!" interrupted Diego.

"Good! So people need to keep their houses as dry as possible. We shouldn't leave wet clothing, wet towels, or wet washcloths, lying around. Good thinking, class!" praised Ms. Matson. "So, if all these suggestions don't work, what else can people do to get rid of cockroaches?"

"Ooh! Ooh!" All the students wanted to speak.

"People use *poison*!" many shouted.

"Some people *spray* poison!" others added.

"You can buy those little Roach Motels, where cockroaches can check in, but never check out!" said Emerald. Everyone laughed. They had all heard those commercials.

"Some people call for *exterminators!*" yelled Carson. The class looked at him again. So did Zak. "What? *What?*" Carson demanded, looking around. No one could believe what they were hearing from him today.

"Right!" said Ms. Matson. "Many people use poisons to kill cockroaches. So why doesn't this always work? For a while, the cockroaches seem to be gone. Then they come back again. What happened?"

"Much later, other cockroaches could move into the house," suggested Bella.

"Good reasoning," said Ms. Matson. "The poison could have faded, or lost its strength, after some time goes by." She paused. "Anything else?" Everyone was quiet.

"Here's another reason," she said. "Sometimes a special poison might kill off almost all of the cockroaches. But a few do not even get sick from that poison. They are *resistant* to it. It doesn't bother them. So they carry on their lives as before. Then those cockroaches have babies. And their babies—the nymphs—will also be *resistant* to that same poison. That particular poison will not hurt them, either. And, because cockroaches lay so many eggs, and they hatch so fast, there will soon be lots of cockroaches around again."

"So, that's why scientists keep making new poisons," said Jamez, "because cockroaches become *resistant* to the old poisons. The old poisons don't bother them anymore."

"Scientists study cockroaches to make new poisons and traps," added Tony.

"And doctors study cockroaches to see why they have lived for so long," said Willow. "I hope they find out."

"And here's another reason that most people never even consider," Ms. Matson said, as the children leaned forward in their seats. "Let's think back to the other day. This is going to take some hard thinking. Now, what did we learn about cockroach antennae?"

"Feel, smell, taste," everyone chanted.

"Super!" smiled Ms. Matson. "Now, about the sense of taste…" She paused. "Where is the antennae located? Is it inside or outside the body?"

"Outside!" Everyone agreed.

"Right! Soooo, if the antennae tastes some poison, is the poison *inside* the body?"

"No!" the class said together.

"Will the cockroach get sick?"

"No!"

"If the cockroach is smart, will it eat or swallow the poison?"

"NO!"

"If you could taste poison on the outside of your body, would *you* put it inside your body?"

"NO!" The whole class was astonished that cockroaches had this ability.

"Can you see that this is *another* way that cockroaches can avoid being killed?"

"Yes!"

"Wow! That's really smart," said Scotty.

"Ms. Matson, can we cross out Question #IV now?" asked Willow.

"Please? We know the answers now," everyone begged.

IV. ~~If everyone tries to get rid of them, why are so many cockroaches still around?~~

The class was thrilled to see the big, fat, black line marked through Question IV. "Hooray!" some shouted, while others gave a silent cheer by waving their hands back and forth in the air, and some boys pumped their fists.

Turning back to face the students, Ms. Mason asked, "If *you* were a cockroach, and you tasted some poison, or got a tiny whiff of poison, would you stick around?"

"NOOOOO!"

"So, what would you do?" she continued.

"Run away!"

"Boogie on out of there!"

"Vamous!"

"Run for your lives!"

"Head for the hills!"

"Hit the road, Jack!"

The students giggled, as they had all had the same thought, but they expressed it differently. Suddenly there was a lot of commotion, as they all got the same idea, all at once, again.

"Ms. Matson, Ms. Matson!"

"Maybe that's why all the cockroaches came out of our drain..."

"That's why they all came out at the same time!"

"Maybe they were trying to get away from some poison..."

"Maybe Mr. Mayo tried to poison the cockroaches!"

"Because of our CRUNCHING PARTY!"

"Aha!" shouted Ms. Matson.

The students were all giving each other high-fives, and congratulating themselves.

"Of course! That makes sense!"

"Why else would hundreds of cockroaches shoot out of our drain at the same time?"

"They had to be afraid of something!"

"Why else would they come out in the daytime?"

"Yeah! They had to be afraid of something!"

Room 8 was so excited. Everyone wanted to talk with Mr. Mayo about the situation. Everyone wanted to be the one to have the answer first.

RING! School was out for the day, so the children all ran off to the playground, to hunt for Mr. Mayo.

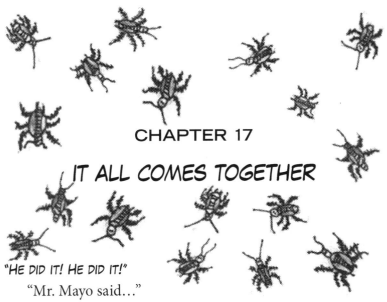

CHAPTER 17

IT ALL COMES TOGETHER

"HE DID IT! HE DID IT!"

"Mr. Mayo said…"

"Mr. Mayo *did* try to poison the cockroaches!"

"The cockroaches were running *away* from the poison!"

The next morning, the students in Room 8 were in an uproar. When Ms. Matson opened the classroom door, much talking and arm waving could be seen.

"All right! All right! Settle down," laughed Ms. Matson. "I can see that many of you have talked with Mr. Mayo, either yesterday afternoon, or this morning." Everyone nodded their heads up and down. "Quiet, please. Now, take your seats, and one at a time, you may tell the class your story."

After the children spoke about their conversations with the janitor, Ms. Matson continued the discussion. "Ahhh," she said. "Now we know why so many cockroaches were racing through the pipes. I think that answers both numbers two and three together. What do you say?" Everyone happily agreed, as Ms. Matson drew big, fat, black, squiggly lines through those questions.

II. ~~Why did the cockroaches come out all at the same time?~~

III. ~~If cockroaches don't like the light, why did they come out of our sink in the daytime?~~

She paused, before asking a question. "But why did the cockroaches only shoot up out of *our* sink? After all, as you know, every classroom in this school has a sink."

"Oh, no," several children moaned, as some thumped their heads with their hands.

"I thought we were through."

"I thought we had *all* the answers."

Much playful grumbling and complaining could be heard. The students all looked around at each other, making funny faces, and rolling their eyes.

"I really think that this is the only thing that we haven't figured out," said Ms. Matson. "Why did the cockroaches shoot out of Room 8's sink, and no other classroom sinks?"

Hmmmm. The students thought and thought. Several shrugged. "What can we do to find out?" she asked.

"Maybe we need to find out how our sink is *different* from other sinks," said Jamez.

"Good thinking!" said Ms. Matson. "So, how do we find that out?"

"We can look at all the sinks."

"Let's see what makes our sink different."

"Let's go and see for ourselves."

Everyone had an idea.

"Yes," said Ms. Matson. "There's nothing like seeing something with your very own eyes. Observation is important." She paused again. "But we can't *all* go charging into other classrooms. It would be too disruptive." Everyone thought some more.

"But we don't *all* have to go into each room…"

"We could go into different classrooms…"

"If one or two of us go into a room to check out the sink, it wouldn't be too disruptive."

"Aha!" said Ms. Matson. "That sounds like it might work!" Everyone smiled.

"How many classes are at our school?" No one knew, for sure. "Okay. Let's count them." They figured it out together, not counting all the new bungalows, that didn't have classroom sinks.

"Twenty-three!" Everyone yelled.

"So, how are we going to work this?" Ms. Matson asked. "We have seven more students than classrooms, and we've all seen our own sink. So that's really eight more students than we need."

So they added the Nurse's room, the cafeteria, and three Specialists' rooms, the Preschool, Mr. Mayo's room, the Teacher's Rooms, and the library.

"That makes even more rooms to check out." How confusing!

"Now, we have more rooms than we have students," sighed Ms. Matson. Groans could be heard.

"Then *you* can check out all the Teacher's Rooms, Ms. Matson!" said Bella.

"Yeah! Then all of us would have one sink each," said Tony.

"All right!" said Ms. Matson. "That's perfect! After all, I *am* learning right along with all of you, so I should be a part of this, too."

Everyone was pleased that each person would be able sink around the school. Smiles and high-fives were seen all around the room.

During recess, all the Teachers' Rooms and Boys' and Girls' Lavatories were checked. When the class began again, as fast as the students were assigned room numbers, they left to quietly inspect those sinks. They came back to Room 8 in groups of twos, threes, and fours. They were discussing what they had observed. Nothing seemed *unusual* about the sinks. No one could see any differences.

"Well, this is really peculiar," said Ms. Matson, as she walked to the back of the room. "Come and join me, class. Let's all look at our sink together, and see if we can see something out of order. Maybe, if we have the other sinks fresh in our minds, we can come up with something." The students bunched up around the sink and cupboard area.

Everyone just stared. Hmmmm. None of the students could see anything out of order. Neither could Ms. Matson. She frowned.

"Well, let's try this," she suggested. "I will point to separate parts of the sink area, and you see in your mind, if your sink looks the same as this one. Ready?"

She pointed. "Were your hot and cold handles any different?"
"Noooo," everyone said.
She pointed again. "Was your faucet different than this one?"
"Noooo," they repeated.
"Was the sink drain hole any different?"
"Noooo," again, shaking their heads back and forth.
"Then what could be different?"

Hmmmm. Everyone stared some more. Quietly. Thinking. Then, the answer seemed to hit all at the same time.

"Ms. Matson, Ms. Matson..."

"The rubber stopper..."

"My sink had a regular sink plug..."

"My sink had a metal stopper..."

"Our drain has a rubber drain cover!"

"Metal!"

"Room 18 had a metal drain stopper!"

"So did Room 24!"

"So did..."

What a jumble of voices! Every student was then questioned, one at a time.

"Did the sink you checked out have a metal or a rubber drain cover?" Everyone answered that the other sinks had built-in metal drain plugs. Those were already built inside the drains, and were always *closed* when not in use. Room 8 was the only classroom that had a rubber water-stopper.

"Oh, my goodness," said Ms. Matson. "I forgot all about that!" She shook her head. "Years ago, when I first moved into Room 8, the metal drain plug was broken. It leaked so badly that it never held water in the sink for any length of time. It was so *frustrating!*" she wailed, as everyone giggled. "So I finally just threw it away!" she laughed. "I bought a flat, rubber drain cover as a cheap replacement, so water would remain in the sink. Most people use these flat, rubber covers for bathtub or sink drains." More giggles were heard, as she shook her head. "I didn't even remember that, it happened so long ago." She shook her head again, and added, "Now I know to always keep the rubber cover *over* the drain!"

The class was laughing and joking and having a good time. The whole mystery was finally solved! The cockroaches *couldn't* have come out of the pipes into any other school sinks, because the metal drain plugs blocked their way. Only Room 8 had a rubber stopper. And it always sat on top of the sink counter, next to the handles, with a bar of soap sitting on top of it. The flat, rubber stopper was only placed over the drain hole when someone actually needed to fill the sink with water.

Finally, everyone was satisfied that they knew the answers to all of the seven questions the class had asked. Ms. Matson grabbed the big, fat, black, felt pen, and scribbled a line through the last unanswered question, as the children clapped.

I. Why did the cockroaches come out of our drain, and not other classrooms?

Then Ms. Matson showed the original butcher paper chart, on which were recorded the facts that the children knew. Beside it, she tacked up a rewritten chart, that *added* all of the new facts the students found about those items. The two charts looked very different. They compared the two charts. The class was amazed to see how much they had learned together.

THINGS WE KNOW ABOUT COCKROACHES

(1)   Cockroaches are insects, with three body parts (head, thorax, and abdomen).

(2)   Most cockroaches are black and brown. Others are brightly colored.

(3)   Most cockroaches have two pair of wings, but not all fly. Females have smaller wings.

(4)   Cockroaches have wide, flat, soft, shiny, oval-shaped bodies.

(5)   Cockroaches have six legs, covered with tiny hairs, and tiny claws on their feet.

(6)   Cockroaches have tiny heads, protected by a shield.

(7)   Cockroaches have two large eyes. Some have simple eyes, and others have compound eyes with 2000 lenses (like little eyes packed closely together). Humans have two lenses.

(8)   Cockroaches have mouths that chew sideways.

(9)   Cockroaches have two long antennae, for feeling, smelling, and tasting.

(10)   Cockroaches have tiny brains. But they can learn and adapt.

(11)   Cockroaches have a heart that stretches down its back, with 13 chambers. Humans have only four chambers.

(12)   Cockroaches have clear or white blood.

(13)   Cockroaches are worldwide pests, throughout history.

(14)   Cockroaches run very fast, over three miles an hour. They can run faster than most humans.

(15) Cockroaches are hard to step on, because they sense air movement.
(16) Cockroaches hide in the daytime, to be safe from predators.
(17) Cockroaches do not like the light, except the Asian cockroach.
(18) Cockroaches come out in the dark. They are nocturnal.
(19) Some cockroaches live indoors, especially in kitchens and bathrooms, and around water pipes.
(20) Most cockroaches live outdoors in the tropics.
(21) Cockroaches are closely related to grasshoppers, crickets, katydids, and others.
(22) Cockroaches are the oldest kind of insect, living over 350 million years.

Midmorning the next day, Ms. Matson brought out a stack of 6-packs of raisins. When she passed out the little red boxes to each student, they instantly knew that it was time for a cockroach test. This was a test that they didn't have to study for. Cockroaches were too interesting to forget! Ms. Matson always said that raisins give a quick energy burst. She said that raisins helped with concentration and memory. So everyone's confidence was high. As she passed out the tests, she encouraged all by simply saying, "Do your best!" and "Show what you know!" All were eager to do just that.

During the last hour of the day, Ms. Matson made an announcement: It came as no surprise that every student got an A! Of course! They were all cockroach *experts* by now! They had pooled their knowledge. "See?" she said. "We learn faster in groups, and it's easier when we're having fun." After all, when people are excited about a subject, they don't even realize how much they are learning.

Ms. Matson always said that it is important to recognize one's achievements. She often said that everyone needed to celebrate their day-to-day victories. So, with smiles and good spirits, everyone patted themselves on the back, to show their satisfaction for a job well down. They were proud of their accomplishments. Afterwards, they offered congratulations to their classmates all around, by throwing high-fives, flying chest bumps, and doing little Snoopy happy dances. Then Par-ty time!

About 15 minutes before school let out, Ms. Matson said that Diego had something to share. To the great surprise of everyone, Diego brought a guitar to the front of the room. The children were so excited! No one even knew that he could play an instrument. He silently placed the strap around his neck, while everyone watched, wide-eyed.

As he began softly strumming his guitar, he began talking. "Here's another history story," he began. "Many years ago, there was a revolution in Mexico. During that war, there was a famous hero called Pancho Villa. He had a big, *old* carriage that was always breaking down. When he went around, from place to place, to visit his soldiers, a wheel kept breaking off his carriage. The soldiers nicknamed his carriage, "La Cucaracha." That means The Cockroach, because it kept going, and going, and going. The men would fix it, and it kept on moving, just like a cockroach. It wouldn't stop. It wouldn't die!" Diego explained, as he kept on strumming.

"So someone made up a song about it. The song says that the cockroach has lost one of its six legs, and it is struggling to walk with only five legs. Over the years, the song has become famous all over the world. People have changed the words many times, in many ways, for many different reasons. It is very popular."

The students couldn't believe what they were seeing. They couldn't believe what they were hearing, as he began to *sing* "La Cucaracha." When he was finished, everyone clapped and cheered. The class went wild!

"Awesome!"

"Sweet!"

"Cool!"

"Bravo!"

"Muy Bueno!"

And Diego smiled.

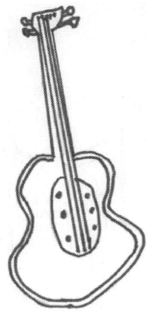

VOCABULARY WORDS

Do you know what do these words mean?

insect   pest
nocturnal   species
copyright page   cerci/cercus
vibrations   spiracles
nymphs   adapt
molts/molting   resistant
common   habitat
antenna/antennae   feelers
infested/infestation   scavenger
observe/observation   compound
egg purse   hatch
ootheca

COCKROACH DIAGRAM

Can you name the main body parts of a cockroach?

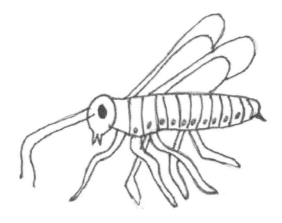

MORE INTERESTING FACTS ABOUT COCKROACHES

(1) History shows that cockroaches were once considered to be honored guests in European houses. It was the custom to release them in new homes. Yikes!

(2) Instead of bones inside their bodies, cockroaches have an exoskeleton, on the outside of their bodies. It is a hard shell that protects them like a shield or a suit of armor.

(3) Cockroaches have small heads. Although they are fast learners, their brains are not as important to them as they are to humans. If they lose their heads, they can live for a week, but then they need water and have no way to drink it, so they will die.

(4) A cockroach heart is long and thin, like a tube, that runs down the middle of the back. Cockroach blood does not carry oxygen, like human blood does. It is a white or clear liquid that sloshes around freely in cockroach bodies. Unlike humans, they have no blood vessels.

(5) Cockroaches have two eyes that are not as useful as their antennae. Human eyes have only one lens each; the cockroach has 2,000 lenses each. While human eyes can see the light of a single candle from the distance of 10 miles, cockroaches can see all around them at the same time, but they do not have sharp vision. Being nocturnal, they can see quite well in semi-darkness, and in green light, but they can't see anything in red light. They are thought to be colorblind.

(6) Cockroaches have strong mouthparts, for biting, chewing, and licking. More taste buds are on four small feelers around their mouths, called palpi. They are like little fingers, two on each side of the mouth, to help them feel and taste the food, before the cockroach eats it.

(7) Most adult cockroaches have two pairs of wings; the front pair are strong and leathery, and are folded over the delicate back wings to protect them. Many cockroaches that can fly have beautiful see-through wings. But they are not good fliers, looking more like grasshoppers hopping.

(8) Cockroach bodies are coated with wax, so they are waterproof, and can slip through tiny cracks easily.

(9) Cockroaches have six hairy legs, with 18 knees. The knees also act like ears, which can hear very soft sounds.

(10) Cockroaches are speedy. Cockroaches are one of the fastest runners in the insect world. It is said that they can run 10 times faster than humans. Some can run about 50 body lengths per second!

(11) Cockroaches have two claws on each foot, with sticky pads, so they can climb straight up walls and smooth surfaces. Even more taste buds are on the bottoms of their feet.

(12) Cockroaches can swim, and can hold their breath, anywhere from 7 to 45 minutes. They swim up drainpipes into sinks and bathtubs.

(13) Cockroaches spend 75% of their time either resting or hiding. They can remain in the same position for up to 18 hours. A couch potato, for sure!

(14) Cockroaches spend a lot of time cleaning themselves, much like a cat.

(15) If seen during the day, it is because their hiding places are overcrowded, due to a large population, or there is a shortage of food or water. Or their dwelling is being fumigated.

(16) Male cockroaches weigh less than female cockroaches, so they can fly and flee faster.

(17) The female Madagascar Hissing Cockroach only mates once, and has three litters a year, each and every year thereafter. She is pregnant for life. Horrors!

(18) Some people get allergies, skin rashes, asthma, or breathing problems from just being around cockroaches. People can get watery eyes and shortness of breath just from being where cockroaches have been.

(19) Cockroaches are insects that belong to the family named Blattaria (which means to "shun the light."), even though the Asian Cockroach flies *toward* the light.

(20) Cockroaches have more muscles than humans. But if a cockroach accidently falls on its back, it can't turn itself over, if there is nothing to grab onto. And it will die.

(21) Some colleges have cockroach races. Get ready, Get set, Go! Sometimes the cockroaches will even pull tiny toy tractors (they can pull more than 20 times their own weight). Several countries share in the fun. Australia holds a yearly cockroach racing competition (on January 26th, Australia Day). Many people bet on cockroach races, just like horse races.

(22) Many years ago in New York, there was an infestation of German Cockroaches on the city buses. So the Manhattan Transit Authority decided to fumigate their entire fleet of 4,500 buses, every two weeks. *Can you imagine?*

(23) You might have a perfectly clean house, but if it is old, watch out! In 1982, a German Cockroach infestation in the House of Representatives, in Washington, D.C., was so bad that experts were called in. It seems that those cockroaches were resistant to all the pesticides being used. They were extremely tough! (Those hardy cockroaches may still be there. *Who knows?)*

(24) One University of New Mexico Ph.D. candidate, Heidi Hopkins, thought that cockroaches were getting bad media coverage. She thought that the public had some strange notions about cockroaches. And she was concerned that scientists hadn't paid any attention to cockroaches in almost 100 years. So she studied them for four years. In February, 2014, she announced that she had discovered 39 new cockroach species in the surrounding deserts. Wow! She says that humans could learn a lot about survival from cockroaches.

(25) Some people keep cockroaches as pets.

(26) Some people like to eat cockroaches. Others like to drink cockroach tea. Ick!

WHAT'S GOOD ABOUT COCKROACHES

(1) Cockroaches are good for the environment. They make the soil better for plants and animals. They break up dead leaves and animal droppings. They clean up the world, like vacuum cleaners. They are like the earth's garbage disposals. This may be why there are so many of them. Cockroaches are nature's recyclers. Biologists say that if cockroaches were to become extinct, it would have a big impact on the health of forests, and all the species that live there. See their role and value in nature.

(2) Cockroaches are a part of the food chain. They eat other insects that are harmful to humans, like flies, wasps, termites, and mosquitoes. Then, in turn, they are an important food source for large centipedes, parasitic wasps, spiders, reptiles, amphibians, fish, birds, bats, animals, and some humans. Understand and appreciate their role in the web.

(3) Certain cockroach species pollinate flowers in the tropics, just like bees.

(4) History tells us that cockroaches have been used as medicine for centuries. Scientists are now studying cockroaches for various medical reasons: everything from blot clots, to T.B., to heart disease. Cockroaches are considered to be the best choice for dangerous bacterial infections (like E. coli and staph infections). Do you know what's in your cough medicine?

(5) Cockroach farms are now big business in China. Cockroaches are raised, like chickens. Then they are dried, ground up into powder, and sold to drug companies. Later, the powder is made

into pills. Cockroach medicine is considered to be a miracle drug, because it can cure a number of ailments. It appears to work faster than other medicines, and has no harmful side effects.

(6) Scientists are studying cockroach hearts, to make better artificial hearts for humans. Cockroaches have 13 heart chambers, and humans have only four. So if something happens to a couple of cockroach heart chambers, it doesn't have a problem. But if something happens to human heart chambers, there is a *big* problem.

(7) Cockroaches are survivors. Scientists are studying the effects of chemicals on cockroach nerves, as they have better defense mechanisms than humans. They are becoming stronger and stronger, learning to transform toxins, over and over again.

(8) Cockroaches are tough little critters. They have a much higher ability to withstand radiation—from six to 15 times that of humans. Scientists are studying the effects of radiation on cockroaches to see why they are so hardy a species.

(9) U.S. Geological scientists checked to see if cockroaches extreme sensitivity to vibration could make them useful as earthquake predictors. American Cockroaches *did* show increased activity just prior to small California earthquakes. But it was found to be not long enough in advance to be helpful or effective.

(10) Cockroaches are being used in experiments in space, to study the effects of longterm space travel. So far, so good.

(11) Scientists are studying cockroach regeneration. If a cockroach accidently loses a mouthpart, antennae, or leg, it can grow a new one, somewhat like when a lizard loses its tail, and grows a new one. Or like starfish that can grow a new arm. Or sharks that can replace lost teeth.

(12) Electrical engineers and computer scientists are studying cockroaches in order to build better robots.

(13) Japanese scientists have developed remote-controlled cockroaches. They have successfully grafted microchips onto their backs, with tiny cameras. These cockroaches might be used as spies. Sounds like a James Bond movie!

We do not have to kiss
frogs, bats, skunks, or cockroaches;
we only need to respect
the "unloved" creatures with which
we share the world.

INDEX

Art Index

The black and white sketches were provided by the winners of *The Cockroach Invasion* Art Contest. The students were from different schools in different cities.

- Stomping tennis shoes, p. 4: Sawyer Grace Grijalva, age 9
- Sink, p. 6: Armani Magana, age 12
- Long antennae, p. 23: Erin Hill, age 10
- A jumble of pipes, p. 26: Mae Cohen, age 9
- Cockroach diagram, p. 29: Kate Elizabeth Kotlyar, age 9
- Dinosaur, p. 31: Sean Jooseung Lee, age 9
- Grasshopper, p. 33: Diego Matthew DeCarlo, age 9
- Wooden sailing ship, p. 36: Morgan Martinez, age 9
- American Cockroach, p. 45: Morgan Martinez, age 9
- Maderia Cockroach, p. 46: Ashlee Martinez, age 9
- Asian Cockroach, p. 47: Eric Kim, age 10
- Cockroach, p. 54: Elliot Navabian, age 10
- Elephant, p. 60: Giovani Magana, age 9
- Puffs of wind, p. 65: Temmie Park, age 9
- Girl's purse, p. 75: Miranda Speirs, age 8
- Molting, p. 76: Clement Niali Murphy, age 10
- Garlic Bulb, p. 82: Giovanni Magana, age 9
- Guitar, p. 100: Morgan Martinez, age 9
- All chapter titles and page number cockroaches: Joshua Ariel Perez, age 9.

A special thanks is extended to

Elizabeth Mary Clements Call,

Art teacher at
Horace Mann School, Beverly Hills, CA
for her
enthusiastic support and encouragement
in this cockroach project.

About the Author

"Books are my life!" says Dr. Sherry L. Meinberg. "I read books, I write books, I edit books, I share books. I eat, sleep, and breathe books."

When she retired from teaching in public schools, Dr. Meinberg owned over 6,000 children's books. She generally reads a book a day, with three to five being read at the same time. A large mishmash of books are stacked in every room in her house. She regularly donates books to libraries, schools, shelters, and individuals. Even her car license says READ4ME, and its license plate holder says SO MANY BOOKS, SO LITTLE TIME. She absolutely loves storytelling, and has carried on a lifelong love affair with the printed word. Books are a source of joy for her. She is a true bibliophile.

Dr. Meinberg later became a core adjunct university professor, as well as a supervisor of student teachers. She retired again, after realizing that she had been teaching for a total of 50 years! She continues to be a speaker for various groups, conferences, and conventions.

Dr. Meinberg has been featured on local, national, and international radio and television shows, as well as newspapers, magazines, and the Internet. To date, she has been honored with 84 awards. This is her eleventh nonfiction book. She is all about raising awareness and opening doors. She is all about getting the word out.

The Cockroach Invasion is a true story.
It actually happened in
the author's
third grade classroom.

If you would like to read
more science/mystery books
featuring the
further adventures of students in Room 8,
which would you like?

The Missing Experiment
The Footprint Phantom
The Tree Bridge
The Angry Ants
The Volcano Explosion
The Snail Race
The Worm Music

Please let the author know.

Dr. Sherry L. Meinberg encourages your feedback.
Your comments, stories, and questions
are most welcome:
sherrymeinberg@verizon.net

COCKROACH CATASTROPHE!

The third graders are in for an exciting and scary experience, as cockroaches take over their classroom. How will they act? What will they do? What would you do? What will they discover about cockroaches?

Nobody loves a cockroach! They make nasty houseguests; the ick factor is very high. But most cockroaches live outdoors and never come in contact with humans. *The Cockroach Invasion* challenges our assumptions and raises awareness about cockroaches and the role they play in our ecosystem. It expands readers' minds and stimulates their imaginations, while contributing to the appreciation of biodiversity. It teaches readers to think twice about underloved yet necessary creatures.

The Cockroach Invasion entertains and informs. It is a delightful read for all ages, stunning in its underlying messages: self-reliance, open-mindedness, and respec for all creatures with which we share our world. No matter how you feel about cockroaches, you are guaranteed to find them fascinating!

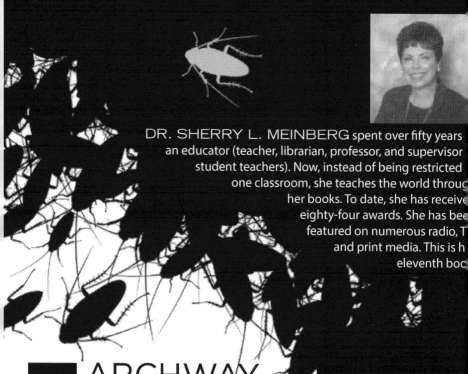

DR. SHERRY L. MEINBERG spent over fifty years an educator (teacher, librarian, professor, and supervisor student teachers). Now, instead of being restricted one classroom, she teaches the world throug her books. To date, she has receive eighty-four awards. She has bee featured on numerous radio, T and print media. This is h eleventh boc

ARCHWAY
PUBLISHING